Life Is Just a
Bowl of Kumquats

Life Is Just a Bowl of Kumquats

TWILA VAN LEER

Saturday Review Press • New York

Published simultaneously in Canada by
Doubleday Canada Ltd., Toronto.

Library of Congress Catalog Card Number: 77-154271

ISBN 0-8415-0142-4

Saturday Review Press
230 Park Avenue, New York, New York 10017

Printed in the United States of America

Design by Margaret F. Plympton

Contents

Life Is Just a
Bowl of Kumquats

How It All Began

We didn't always have nine children, you know.

Oh no. I remember distinctly back in the olden days when we were very first married and had only one child.

I married Gerda and her daddy when she was about six years old. It was kind of a package deal.

And then one evening we were just sitting around the living room not doing much of anything, when all of a sudden—whap, whap, pow, zonk, zing, zing, zing.

There they all were: Alan, Steven, Laurel, Melinda, Brian, Russell and Valerie.

At least it seems it happened that fast. I know that in harking back, I never can hark a time that we didn't have wall-to-wall kids.

I realize that two whaps, a pow, a zonk and three zings (plus Gerda) only add up to eight, but I'm saving the ninth one for a big surprise later on.

As a matter of fact, as the little brothers and sisters kept arriving with such startling regularity, it became a matter of amazement even to our older children. I could almost hear them thinking, "Gee whiz. How does Mom *do* that?"

Eventually they quit thinking it and asked right out loud.

Dirk and I had decided right from the outset that when the questions regarding the birds and the bees started arriving, we would meet them calmly, in a straightforward manner, evading nothing and giving the children answers straight from the shoulder.

Only we didn't anticipate them coming so very soon.

When Alan and Steve were just five and six, Dirk brought home some salmon from the nearby river, where the poor fish had been struggling upstream to do their thing and then to die happy.

It certainly seemed like a ridiculous custom to me. But then—to each its own, I suppose.

As Daddy went about cleaning the fish so that we could smoke them and tuck them away in the larder against winter's chill, he found that many of them still were laden with their burden of eggs and sperm.

"Oho!" thought he. "I'll raise myself some salmon."

So he put some little roly-poly yellowish-orange eggs in a peanut-butter jar, added several spoonfuls of the male contribution and sat back waiting for the fish to hatch.

As usual, the audience participation was enthusiastic and verbal. Questions fell like summer rain.

Dirk explained patiently that the eggs must be fertilized in order for the little fishes to grow, and the subject appeared to be closed.

(Obviously the little fishes needed a few other things which they never got, for in a few days the peanut-butter jar scummed over and the smell of stagnation filled the kitchen. I gave up plans for smoking the crop and chucked the jar into the garbage.)

For several days after the fish-fertilizing episode, Steve wandered around the house with a distant look on his face that meant the cogs inside his little noggin were turning double time. I kept waiting for the big question to pop.

Finally it did.

"Mother," he questioned as I stood busy at the ironing board, "if babies have to be fertilized, who fertilized Russell?"

Calmly, in a straightforward manner, evading nothing and giving him the answer straight from the shoulder, I said, "Go ask your father."

Then I listened as he went into the living room where Daddy was engrossed in a football game via television. He posed the same question.

Dirk, bless his heart, rose to the occasion nobly. Without embarrassment or bushbeating, calmly, in a straightforward manner, evading nothing, he gave the boy an answer straight from the shoulder.

"Go ask your mother."

You know, this little ditty about the stork has some distinct advantages.

In Holland, Dirk's homeland, they have their own version of the tale, in which babies are found inside cabbage plants.

Why not? It has some advantages over the conventional method. I've long maintained that there should be an easier way to populate the world. True, we may have to give up corned beef and cabbage and coleslaw, but that's a trifling price to pay.

Of course, if you can hold off any explanations anent the peopling of the world until your little shavers reach kindergarten age, it's all taken care of for you.

I remember Maximillian.

Maximillian was a big white rabbit who shared a classroom with Alan and some twenty other kindergarteners. There seemed to be some question as to just what sort of rabbit Maximillian might be.

The kindergarten teacher had expressed these doubts in a large poster-board story which was hung above Maximillian's cage.

Maximillian is our rabbit. We do not know if
Maximillian is a father rabbit or a mother rabbit.
Maximillian spent the Christmas holidays with
Arnold's rabbits. Soon we will know if Maximillian
is a father rabbit or a mother rabbit.

On the day I visited the kindergarten, Maximillian had
just given birth to four pinkish little babies. Apparently
the weekend with Arnold's rabbits had been a rouser.

Just another of those cases where only the hare-dresser
knew for sure, I guess.

Since those good old days, we've had ample opportunity
to delve into the subject of sex with the children, and I
feel we've established a fair amount of rapport with them
in this area.

Sometimes they even deign to tell us what *they* know,
which is considerable.

Of course, things used to be much more simple back
before the big Sexual Revolution.

I don't think sex itself has changed so much, but consider the plight of the poor tomato.

Scientists are bent on taking all of the romance out of
the life of the lowly love apple, at the same time compli-
cating things for well-meaning parents.

You may have heard about it. They've developed a
method called hydroponics in which they grow perfectly
lovely tomatoes, bypassing all of the old standard
procedures.

All this without so much as by-your-leave from the
tomatoes themselves.

It used to be we could tell our children a pretty tale of
bees flitting through the tomato patches, spreading pollen
right and left, causing hay fever and pollination.

That's what makes the little tomatoes (or flowers or
what-have-you) grow, we told them.

Now, by jingies, they have eliminated the middleman, or
bee, as the case may be, and have some totally impersonal

technician tiptoing through the tomatoes shocking them with some sort of device that jolts them into producing whether they like it or not. (And as a mother, might I say it's enough of a jolt to find out you're producing, without all that other stuff going on.)

Think of it. Hundreds of hives full of unemployed bees, sitting around twiddling their antennae and participating in endless buzz sessions about how it used to be in the good old days when they were valued and useful members of Mother Nature's family.

In addition, the scientists have decided that good old water and sunshine can no longer be trusted to do the job. The new tomatoes thrive on a chemical diet.

And we've all been made well aware of what happens to little things that take to the chemicals! It's addiction-ho!

There's a whole new crop of drug-befogged, socially misfit tomatoes coming up, and no one cares except myself and the catsup people.

The scientists are not going to stop at tomatoes, either. They're digging into the private lives of all the plants, rending them from their native soil and putting them into sterile hothouses where they'll never know the hum of the bee, the gentle kiss of rain or the soft caress of the summer sunshine.

I'll bet they go so far as to produce a pea plant that doesn't have a pod to pea in.

It sure loses something in the telling, compared to the birds and bees bit.

Ah, well, however you explain it, it's whap, pow, zonk and zing all over the place, and children just go on getting born every day.

And isn't that nice, after all?

Absolutely, Positively the Last—Probably, Maybe

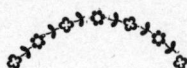

Back in the early fall of 1967, when I was still waddling around lumpy and grumpy waiting for Valerie to arrive, I read something in the newspaper that really put a crimp in my gasket.

Some lady had delivered her own baby in the afternoon and was up that evening fixing supper for her husband.

The nerve!

If there's anything I hate, it's a smart-aleck female who makes the rest of us look like a bunch of sissies.

The only thing I hate worse is to have my husband read about these super beings, peering over the top of the newspaper at me with a look that clearly intimates:

"Ha. How could I have been stuck with this obviously inferior hunk of humanity who expects to be run to the hospital for every little thing?" (Little things are all I ever run to the hospital for—little girls, little boys, etc.)

Curses upon all those do-it-yourselfers who sort of knock off their babies between pancakes, like the heroines in the Pearl Buck novels.

Let them make their own deliveries if they want to, but in the interest of us pantywaists who still prefer the hospital trip, let's keep it out of the newspapers, okay?

Of course, I have to admit it makes for a pretty little vignette—the husband coming home from the office to find the little lady, slim as a willow wand, fresh as a daisy and chipper as a chipmunk, popping the steak into the broiler.

He Hi, honey. What's new?

She Not much, dear. I hope you won't mind if dinner is a little late this evening. I had to take out a few minutes this afternoon to have the baby and I'm running a little later than usual.

He Forget it, kid. It only happens once a year or so. Say, new baby, huh? Boy or girl?

She Boy. It's over there in the basket if you'd care to take a look.

A pox on all such people!

Personally, I like to lie around in the hospital for a few days, softly moaning to myself.

Not that I'm in any particular physical discomfort, mind you. It's the thought of all those dirty diapers, sleepless nights and crumbled cookies ahead of me that causes the anguish.

Actually, by the time I'd put in my second week of overtime waiting for Valerie, I'd have settled for having the blinking baby *anywhere.*

I was tired of being behind the eight ball—a clever bit of witticism I used to cajole myself through the wearisome months because this was going to be the eighth child. I find it helps to maintain a sense of humor—if you can find anything funny in an abdomen that resembles Mount Everest before and the Grand Canyon afterward.

We made one dry run to the hospital and after a few

...d home to the accusations of our tribe, who
      promised a new brother or sister and who looked
      at grownups who didn't keep their promises.
   ...elt guilty as well as lumpy and grumpy.

Finally the whole thing took on the aspect of an affair
that is going to last forever and doesn't require any special
attention.

I could hardly bring myself to time the contractions on
the Sunday afternoon when things finally did get under
way. Frankly, I was a little resentful at this intrusion on
my Sunday crossword puzzle.

By the time I had decided that this was the real thing
and that perhaps it would be well to pick up my suitcase
and get on with it, a crisis had arisen.

"Hey, Mom," Alan wanted to know, meandering into
the bedroom, "how do you get a pop bottle off your
thumb?"

This was no idle question; he had a pop bottle dangling
from his thumb.

After trying several times to dislodge it, I felt that it
might be destined to hang from his thumb for some time
to come.

"Get some butter," I suggested. "We'll try greasing it."

We greased it, but the bottle just skidded around and
around and stayed put.

"I think my thumb is swelling," Alan announced with
some perverse satisfaction.

"Neat," I commented, sitting down to wait for a con-
traction to pass. "Look, try some soap."

We slopped up the thumb with soap, which washed away
the butter and not much else.

"Wiggle it up and down and see if you can get some of
the soap down inside," I suggested. "No, no. Not that way.
Try to kind of do it sideways, not just up and down. Can't
you just sort of unscrew it somehow? Here, get me another
bottle and I'll show you how."

By now the bathroom was filled to overflowing with interested spectators, and one of them was happy to run for another bottle. Something like this helped to take the dull edge off a Sunday afternoon. We were only missing Daddy, who still was immersed in the Sunday paper, waiting for me to decide it was time to make the hospital trek.

"All right now." I demonstrated, poking my thumb into the second bottle. "Don't try to pull it straight out. Bend it as much as you can and twist the bottle around so it will come off a little at a time. Like this."

He followed my every move with commendable concentration, and I rejoiced exceedingly as the bottle began to ease itself off his thumb.

That left only one problem. The same process wasn't working for me.

I twisted the bottle one way and then another and pulled and pushed and wiggled, but I still had a bottle on my thumb.

Now that he was rid of his own bottle, Alan was all authoritative suggestion.

"Soap it, Mom," he urged. "That really helps. And don't try to pull it straight out. Bend your thumb and kind of unscrew it."

"Diiirrrk!" I screamed, convinced all of a sudden that my new progeny was going to be the first ever born to a mother whose right thumb was permanently encased in a pop bottle.

Dirk roared into the bathroom, sped no doubt by visions of his offspring being born in the bathtub. "What are you doing?" he demanded when he saw me standing there yanking frantically at the pop bottle.

"I'm doing two things," I snapped. "Getting this bottle off my thumb and having a baby, and I hope they come in that order."

He dropped the paper, latched onto the bottle and gave a

yank that bade fair to relieve me not only of the bottle, but also of all of my fingers, my hand, wrist, elbow and everything else up to and including my shoulder.

"Soap, Dad," Alan cried above the sounds of my own cries of distress. "Use some butter."

"Leave it be! Leave it be!" I shouted. "I'd rather have the bottle than lose an arm!"

Friend husband ignored both the advice and the imploring. Getting a perfectly lovely wrestling grip on my shoulder from behind, he got a death hold on the bottle and pulled again, at the same time twisting my arm in what I felt sure was about three complete turns.

With a resounding *pop,* the bottle flew off and I fell backward against Dirk.

"You've broken my thumb!" I wailed, holding on to that member, which felt as if someone were inflating it.

"Good. It will take your mind off your other troubles," Dirk sympathized. "Come on, let's get going."

Within seconds, Dirk and the suitcase and I were in the car, en route to the hospital to see what God had wrought with this little Number Eight.

Immediately upon arriving, the law of relativity was put into effect.

I believe women the world over may have noticed this phenomenon. It goes something along the lines of "My, doesn't time pass quickly when you're having fun?"

As soon as the formalities of admission were over, a nurse wheeled me away into the inner sanctum where she assured me, as she administered those lovely little prebirth rites, that "You're going to be all through here in no time."

Then our dear old Doctor Bob took his turn at looking over the situation, patted me on the shoulder and joyfully commented that, "We should have that baby here in plenty of time for me to get home and watch the 'Dick Van Dyke Show.'"

Boy, was I relieved.

Then Dirk came in and put in his two-bits' worth.

"Doctor Bob says it won't be long, dear. We're going to have that little girl before you know it."

"My thumb hurts," I responded piteously, and turned my back on him.

"Remember that this is absolutely the last baby," he consoled me. "This is the last trip we'll have to make for this reason. We won't have to go through this again."

"*We* won't?" I snarled. "Oh, hooray, hooray!"

There was no mistaking that sarcasm. Dirk figured if I was just going to be nasty, there wasn't any point in continuing the conversation. He settled down with a magazine and talked with the nurse instead.

"You aren't really calling it quits, are you?" She smiled. "We've gotten kind of used to having you in every so often."

"You bet your life this is quits," Dirk replied. "This is eight, you know. That's a nice round figure to stop on."

"Speaking of nice round figures," I interjected sourly.

"You'll have that figure back any minute now," the nurse concluded after another quick peek. "Let's get the doctor up here and get this show on the road. That didn't take long, did it?"

"No, no. Not at all," I agreed pleasantly, subduing an urge to scream. "Is it still 1967?"

However, even I was forced to admit that it wasn't long thereafter that that most beautiful of sounds filled the delivery room. A pig-squealy little cry announced that another human life had been launched.

"Twila, you have a beautiful little daughter," Doctor Bob proclaimed. "She's going to be a movie star, I can tell."

That dear man. What a bedside manner.

"Oooooh," I moaned. "I wanted a little girl so badly."

"You *have* a little girl, Mrs. Van Leer," the nurse repeated, in an attempt to get through the fog.

"I know," I sobbed. "I wanted a little girl so badly."

She gave up. There's no explaining new mothers.

Within a short time, they had wheeled me down the hall and tucked me into a fresh bed, just in time for bedtime, I might say, which shows tremendous foresight on my part.

Little Eight Ball was a darling tousle-headed girl, God was in His heaven and all was right with my world.

As I dozed off, I could hear Dirk out in the hallway telling another nurse that "It really is great, but this time for sure, it's Absolutely the Last."

'Tis the Season for Such Folly

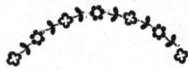

When the frost is on the pumpkin,
My fodder goes in shock
And my mudder doesn't like it either.

Have you ever had the feeling that you were standing around with confetti still in your ears from New Year's, when all of a sudden another Christmas was upon you?

It happens to me all the time.

The first few weeks after we brought Valerie home from the hospital were spent in conducting guided tours around the bassinet, with the tour guide trying desperately to keep the sniffles and sneezes directed in the other direction.

If she "boo-ed" there were from six to eight ardent admirers on hand to pick her up before she "hoo-ed." For several weeks, she was the only infant in town who had her diapers changed when she wasn't even wet.

Then the novelty wore off and Mother was left to cope with diapers both wet and otherwise.

Simultaneously, while the Halloween pumpkin wilted in

the basement and with the Thanksgiving turkey carcass still taking up space in the refrigerator, Christmastime suddenly was here again.

Time for the kids to haul out the holly and mangle the mistletoe.

Time for the grand old songs and the favorite stories.

Brian wandered around the house mumbling his own particular version of "The Night Before Christmas:"

> Away to the window he flew like a flash,
> Tore open the shutters and threw up on the sash.

By the fifteenth of December, I was standing around knee-deep in cooky dough, popcorn balls, homemade candy and last-minute sewing, realizing once again that I had waited too long to start early.

I wondered if Dirk would mind if I gave him the sweater I'd started knitting for the past Father's Day—with one sleeve. Probably he'd be snide.

He was still being snide about the sweater I made him for Christmas a couple of years before which somehow never did get the pocket lining sewed down. The lining still wasn't sewed down, and it seemed a good prospect to bet that the sweater would wear out before the lining did get sewed down.

It was ridiculous, anyhow, to be so picky. No one could tell by looking that the lining wasn't sewed down, and no one had any business putting his hand inside the pocket except Dirk and me, and we both knew that the lining wasn't sewed down.

Of course, if he was going to insist on putting things in there . . .

While I was at home busy trying to beat the December twenty-fifth deadline, the teachers at school also were busy whipping into shape their annual programs which would keep me from beating my deadline.

By the time the schools and the church all took a whack

at it, I figured we spent approximately enough time during the season sitting through programs to finish the sleeve of one sweater.

However, I wouldn't have missed the programs.

I've always been struck by the fact that my children stand out so in a crowd.

And by the fact that so few other people appear to have noticed this phenomenon.

Well. Sometimes they do. Like the time Melinda showed up wearing a big hair bow she'd improvised on the sly from one of Daddy's ties.

It was hard to miss her, too, because she sang the Christmas songs with such gusto that almost invariably she was still singing even after the accompanist had given up and quit.

I wished she hadn't stood out in the crowd quite so much.

Brian also had his day in the spotlight.

As a kindergartener, he was appearing in his first production, and he suffered considerably from stage fright, not being quite so flamboyant as Melinda.

"Do I *have* to go to the program?" he asked as we outfitted him in a pair of Laurel's tights for his grand entrance as an elf. When we had them pulled up to his armpits, they fell in folds around his ankles, covering the tops of his shoes.

"Of course you have to go, son," I responded. "All of the children are going and it will be a great program."

"I'll forget all the songs," he wailed, while I tried to stitch the bulk of the leftovers of the tights up around his thighs.

"The teacher will be there to help you," I assured him. "You'll do just fine." I folded the tights around his skinny little waist one more notch and hoped the seams wouldn't show beneath his tunic.

He moped off into the bedroom while I moved on to the

next project, which involved making a "Pin the Star on the Christmas Tree" game for a party Alan and Steve were having down in the basement.

I was stymied, however, due to the lack of a marking pen. I had left mine right on the table, but now it was nowhere to be found.

I looked in all the usual places, and some unusual places, but it hadn't turned up by the time we were due at the kindergarten program.

At least I was fairly certain that in spite of his stage fright, Brian had made it back to school. He'd dragged his red crepe-paper hat through the snow every inch of the way and we followed a bright red trail to the school.

No sooner did the program get under way than I had a sudden inspiration as to where my felt-tipped pen might be. Beyond the shadow of a doubt, it was in Brian's coat pocket.

There he was, standing out in the crowd, the only elf in elfin history with baggy breeches and a severe case of the bubonic plague.

Between the bright black polka dots on his face, the skin glowed rosy and pink where, no doubt, a poor frantic teacher had tried to scrub him into a presentable state.

It was a great performance. Brian fulfilled his own dire prophecies by forgetting the words to all the songs. He just stood there looking pockmarked.

Another holiday moment to remember.

From then until Christmas Eve was just a blur of activity, with cooking, baking, sewing, Christmas carding, parties and all the rest blending and overlapping into a regular frenzy of coming and going.

Then, before you could say Kris Kringle, the big day itself had arrived.

Time once again for our annual Snap and Button Sewing and Christmas Eve Cursing Session.

I sewed the snaps and buttons on new Christmas outfits

for the girls and on doll clothes. Dirk cursed all the put-together toys that Santa Claus dumped every year.

After an exhausting evening of turkey buffet, scripture reciting, carol singing and general joviality with the neighbors and their four children, it was almost too much to ask of mere mortals.

"Why don't you do your Christmas cursing early next year?" I suggested, threading up my needle for the fourth time.

"You know why. There isn't any place to put anything," friend husband replied, looking like a mad machinist sitting on the kitchen floor surrounded by his tools and the parts and pieces from five or six toys.

He was right. Our bed was standing several inches off the floor now, riding a crest of gifts shoved under there for weeks past awaiting the big event. Flat boxes of parts we could accommodate, but finished wagons, bikes, trikes and life-scale doll furniture we could hardly handle.

It was 1:30 A.M.

"I can guarantee I'm not going through this again next year," Dirk stated flatly. It was a direct quote from himself, one year to the date earlier.

"A guy would have to be an engineer to figure some of this stuff out," he said, chasing a screw under the table.

I clucked sympathetically and went on with my sewing.

By 2:30 A.M., miraculously, everything was under the tree and I stood back to admire. When it came right down to it, Christmas was really pretty nice. We dragged ourselves to bed.

At 3 A.M., there was rustling and sneaky sounds in the hallway.

"Go back to bed," Father bellowed. The rustling and sneaky sounds disappeared back into the bedrooms.

At three-thirty, there was whispered consultation, and I knew they were debating who should be sent to ask if they could get up yet.

At 3:45 A.M., Russell appeared at the bedroom door. As the youngest and the erstwhile baby, he had been selected by unanimous acclaim as the delegate least likely to be yelled at.

"I think it must be morning now," he suggested hopefully. It was pitch black outside.

"Go back to bed and stay there," Father roared.

In the end, it was the baby who betrayed us. At 5 A.M., she was ready for her bottle.

At the first whimper, there was immediate response from four different directions.

"Mama, the baby is awake. Is it morning now?"

I know when I'm licked.

"It's morning," I conceded wearily.

The household erupted into a clamorous din, and wrappings flew with gay abandon as the decibel count went up, up, up.

I sat on the couch with Valerie on one arm, her bottle emptying steadily in spite of the mayhem. My lap was filled with two empty spools, some shiny rocks and several wads of wrapping paper, all carefully wrapped in other bits of wrapping paper and put under the tree for me. They were gifts with heart, to Mama with love from Russell.

"They're happy!" Dirk noted with some amazement, surveying his noisy brood from a chair where he slumped, also with a lapful of Yule loot.

"If it would only last," I responded.

If only it could, indeed.

"Dear God," I prayed, hoping that my silent petition could be heard above the uproar. "Let there be peace on earth, good will toward men. And, Lord, if that's too much to ask, let there be peace and good will at least in the Van Leer household until I can get breakfast under way.

"Amen, amen."

For Every Foolish Act, There's a Ridiculous Reason

Many people have wondered why in the ever-loving world the Van Leers decided to adopt a baby when their own Absolutely Last Baby was just a few months old.

As a matter of fact, in looking back, I have difficulty in putting my finger right on the motivating factor. I only recall that at the moment it seemed like a good idea.

Actually, I suppose the whole thing sprang from the fact that I read in the newspaper one day that a young woman had dropped into a local welfare office, deposited her infant on a desk and marched out again with the announcement that she was leaving town and couldn't be bothered with the child.

This isn't an isolated incident, of course. There are thousands of babies born each year who seem somehow to have fallen into the category of human "weeds." There appears to be no place for them, and often they are left to grow rank with no cultivation of any kind, nurtured only by chance bits of sunshine and moisture that happen along.

It has always been a great sadness to me.

With the wonderment of my own recent motherhood still fresh upon me, I suppose I was more impressionable than I might have been at another time. The thought of the abandoned baby stuck with me and kept popping into my mind at odd moments for several weeks.

I didn't realize that the thoughts were leading me toward such drastic action, however. That part of it just kind of sneaked up on me.

For several years, friend husband has gone to a nearby Indian reservation once each month to take care of special X-ray work at the Public Health Service hospital.

So, of course, once each month the children put in a bid for souvenirs from the reservation. I don't know why, because Daddy never had time for gathering goodies on his monthly visits. He never brought anything back, but the kids continued to ask, right on schedule.

One month, just after Valerie was born, I happened to throw my bid into the general clamor.

"Bring back a little papoose," I chirped, and before you knew it, we had begun to adopt an Indian baby.

It wasn't all that simple, of course. Nothing so drastic as dealing with a human life ever is, but it's so impossible to explain that it seems simple on the surface.

I had no idea, to begin with, that Father would go along with another of my harebrained ideas.

However, Dirk has one infallible soft spot, and it has to do with children.

(Remember when he brought home that little four-year-old girl with the terrible speech defect? He found her while traveling his milk route. This was back during the days when the milk route was seeing us through his education, and it was pretty tough sledding. He didn't hesitate, however, to bring her home, a pathetic little specimen who'd been dumped in the lap of one of Dirk's customers, an older woman who loved the child but couldn't cope with her. We'd have adopted this one, too, I suppose, but the mother was unwilling to part with the Aid to Dependent Children income, although entirely willing to part with the child. We sadly turned her back.)

Dirk had also seen many children at the reservation hospital, little weeds who had been abandoned, neglected and otherwise abused. They were awaiting placement in foster homes, adoptive homes or the state orphanage.

When we began seriously to discuss the possibility of adding another child to our own tribe, I think it was this soft spot for youngsters that tripped Dirk up.

On his next trip to the reservation, he discussed the situation with the hospital administrator and said that if they had a baby (girl, please) in the next little while that needed a home, we'd be pleased if they'd consider the Van Leers. The process had begun.

Of course, you just don't do something like this and tell your friends and relatives that it "seemed like a good idea at the moment." You have to have *reasons*.

We had already decided to keep our big secret under wraps until there was something concrete to report, but in the meantime I began to think up explanations to make the whole thing plausible.

I conducted lengthy and imaginary conversations with my good friend Betty.

Me   Well. Would you believe that we've decided to adopt a little Indian baby? *(A lighthearted giggle.)*

Betty   You're nuts.

Me   Not really. You know, except for Gerda, all of the children have come in pairs—Alan and Steven; Laurel and Melinda; Brian and Russell. Now we've got Valerie and she's Absolutely the Last and she's going to have to grow up all alone.

Betty   What do you mean, all alone? She's got seven brothers and sisters. You're nuts.

Me   Well, what I mean is that she doesn't really have a

	partner. She isn't a matched set. And we've got more clothes for her than we've had for the other babies, and it really is a shame not to use them.
Betty	You can give them to the Salvation Army.
Me	Even two babies won't wear them all out. We can give them to the Salvation Army afterward. Gee whiz. There are so many little babies that no one wants. They can't all be placed, especially the Indian babies. They go to orphanages. No child should grow up in an orphanage.
Betty	There are hundreds of couples around who have no other children who want to adopt.
Me	There aren't enough, though. Besides that *(lamely)* it seems like a good idea at the moment.
Betty	You're nuts.

How can you carry on a conversation with someone who just refuses to understand? No, I could see that we'd never be able to explain it.

Once the decision was made, I got a terrible itch to tell someone. I never could rest comfortably with a secret, like Dirk can. I called my mother and hinted that big things were afoot while never letting the cat out of the bag, so that I could honestly report to Dirk that I hadn't said a word.

The next letter I wrote to Mom, I continued to add to her curiosity by writing some clues:

1. We are hiring the children out to do the sound effects for a series of Tarzan movies.

2. We are going to Alaska for the winter so Dirk can do X-ray work at a native fishing village among the Indians.

3. We are adopting triplets.

4. The government of Uganda has offered us a lifetime supply of bananas if we will promise never to tour the country as a family.

Ha! I thought. How very clever. There are clues here

about both adopting and Indians. I'm sure Mother will catch on immediately and I can honestly tell Dirk that I didn't tell her.

Mom wrote back:

"Obviously, the first clue is correct. You're nuts."

Yes, it was going to be very difficult to explain.

In the final analysis, we were forced to resort to the Van Leer Theory of Vanishing Returns to provide plausibility for our actions.

(Note: The Van Leer Theory is not to be confused with the Murphy Theory of Vanishing Returns. Mrs. Murphy was the old Irish washerwoman who first noted that the number of odd socks in any one washing is roughly equal to the number of pairs worn by the combined members of the family during the preceding wash period. Actually, I don't believe Mrs. Murphy was the first to notice this phenomenon, since it doubtless began with Mother Eve, but the washerwoman was the first to state it in mathematical terms. She later developed a companion theory which states that if the odd socks are kept in a warm, dry place such as a box or bag for six months, then discarded, the mates automatically appear within twenty-four hours, keeping the stock of odd socks constant.)

The Van Leer Theory, on the other hand, is based on the premise that if something is not going to matter fifty years from now, there's no point in worrying about it.

In its practical application, it works like this:

If on October 29, 1950, for instance, I leave the dishes in the sink to spend time helping the children to make Halloween cookies, will anyone remember on October 29, 2000, that the dishes went undone? Highly unlikely. However, the children may remember fifty years from now that they made Halloween cookies.

You see how simple it is?

In the matter of adoption, the reasoning went like this:

If in 1968 we adopt a ninth child, thereby doubling the

number of diapers to be washed, meals to be spoon fed, trips to the doctor, cookies crumbled on the floor, etc., etc., ad infinitum, will it really matter in 2018?

Not nearly so much as the fact that we'd have had the association of another unique human being in the give and take of life, which is, after all, the essence of living.

Possibly as a theory it leaves something to be desired, but it will do in a pinch if you can't think of any other reasonable reason for some ridiculous action.

Tepee or Not Tepee

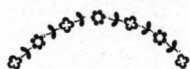

I have often been filled with wonderment that when a person is going about doing something that he feels is, after all, rather stupendous, the world proceeds just the same as if each day were simply a routine old dirt-diapers-dust-dishes and drudgery sort of day.

While we were plumbing the depths, so to speak, of our beings, trying to make a drastic decision, the kids were just clogging the plumbing, as usual.

While we searched our souls, we also searched the house for lost shoes, a pair of scissors, the baby's pacifier, schoolbooks (which had in each instance been left *right where they belonged*) and a thousand other items badly in need of being searched for.

Life went on just the same as if we weren't attempting to make up our minds as to whether or not we should take on the joys and woes of another human being in our family.

As I often do when trying to make a decision, I sought mental support by trying to visualize how some famous person, older and wiser than I, would look at the same set of facts.

How would William Shakespeare, for instance, approach

this business of debating the wisdom of adopting another child, especially a child of another race, when the house was already filled, as it were, to overflowing?

Should we make a hogan of our homely hovel?

Could our abode abide another personality?

Might not our residence resent another resident with all the resultant equipage?

Shouldst? Couldst? Mightst? I could hear the famed old bard pondering.

"Tepee or not tepee? Whether 'tis nobler in the mind to suffer the slings and arrows of eight outrageous children, or to take another in our arms and add to our sea of troubles . . ."

In the end, both Will and I concluded that it was "a consummation devoutly to be wished." My impatience grew with each passing day.

I assumed that once the decision had been made, it was merely a matter of running to the reservation and bringing home the new baby.

As a matter of fact, several months elapsed between the decision and the delivery of the goods.

Time might have hung heavy, had it not been for the children, who did everything they could to keep my days filled with precious little moments.

From the time the weather warmed enough for them to be out and around, they spread out in umpteen different directions looking for something that they could bring home that would relieve me of the tedium of waiting.

I have put it down in my memory as the "Year of the Snake."

I've never considered myself much of a snake charmer, but then the feeling is mutual—snakes don't charm me much either. In fact, my slumbers have oft been disturbed by dreams of snakes standing upright on their tails blocking my pathway when I had important places I needed to be. (I'm sure there must be some psychological significance to these dreams, but I've avoided finding out.)

Anyway, we've gone along all through the years, the snakes and I, operating on the tacit agreement: "You stay out from underfoot and I won't step on you."

When you think of it, though, a snake doesn't really stand as much chance of being trodden underfoot when I'm in the immediate vicinity as he does of being crushed beneath my body when I keel over in a dead faint.

That is why it was so distressing suddenly to find myself living in a veritable snake pit.

It all began on a small scale after the boys had returned one day from a fishing trip with their dad. I noticed Steve sneaking into the bathroom with something, so I went sneaking in behind to find out what he was sneaking about.

I caught him unloading a seven-inch water snake from his pocket into a pop bottle.

I determined not to faint and to be reasonable about the whole thing.

"Let's be fair about this," I told myself, hanging onto the doorknob for support. "It's only a bitty little snake. Perhaps in time I could come to love it."

So I crooked my neck and peered through the pop bottle. The snake crooked its neck clear down to its tail bone, looked right back at me with beady little eyes and stuck out its tongue.

Right then I knew it would never work.

"Out! Out! Out!" I screamed, pointing dramatically toward the bathtub. I didn't dare turn my back on the monster long enough to point to the door.

Steve got the message. He picked up the pop bottle and disappeared around the corner while I tried to wash the prickles off my neck and face with a damp washcloth.

What I had intended was that they take the little nipper down to the river or some other spot approximating its natural habitat.

How great was my joy when Steve came in to report that he'd disposed of it.

"I dumped it in the peppermint bushes behind the house," he said.

How short-lived was my joy. I spent the next few days locked in the house, standing in the center of the living room on one leg with the other foot tucked behind the opposite knee, with both arms folded around my waist, turning constantly to keep a steady surveillance on all entrances and exits.

Gradually I got used to the idea of a snake in the peppermint bushes, howbeit praying all along that the serpent had moved on into the neighbor's yard or something.

But my nerves had not recovered completely before the boys compounded their felony.

It was just a few days later that they came home with the joyous tidings that they had killed a rattlesnake.

"See? Here's the rattlers," Alan announced proudly, ramming the grisly things up to a spot approximately a quarter inch from my nose, where, if I focus properly, I can see, not one, but four of anything. (My children are under the impression that I can't see anything unless it's within batting distance of my eyelashes.)

"You can tell we just killed it, because the meat's still red," he confided. "Steven has the other one."

"The other what?" I screamed, backing against the wall and preparing to defend myself.

"It isn't a rattler," Alan hastened to explain. "It's only a blue racer and it isn't quite dead yet."

"Oh. Well, then," I said, collapsing into a heap on the floor.

"He's going to skin it and make a belt."

I moaned.

For several weeks thereafter, each time I had to go upstairs, I was greeted by the sight of the blue racer and the rattlesnake, skinned and tacked side by side on a board to dry.

They hadn't told me about the rattlesnake skin coming

home along with the rattlers until it was all tacked. I think they gathered from the way I was cringing in a corner shivering and reciting nursery rhymes that I'd had enough for one day without knowing about the rattlesnake skin.

Steve tried to console me.

"You shouldn't be so scared of snakes," he said. "They're good to eat, you know. You fix them just like you do fish. With corn meal."

I repressed the urge to be sick.

That afternoon I went grocery shopping and found that the price of hamburger had gone up ten cents a pound again. Suddenly the thought of snake meat prepared with corn meal flashed into my mind and I began to see the possibilities.

Just imagine the supply aspect alone, I reasoned with myself. If my imagination is any criterion for judgment, snakes are everywhere. There's at least one under every rock and bush, upon each ledge and tree stump and coiled around every wiener roasting stick in the great outdoors.

In the house, there are great herds of them in every closet and at least three under my bed each time I have to haul out at night to refuel the baby's bottle.

"We'd never run out," I mused, standing dejectedly in front of the hamburger.

Think of all the yummy ways I could prepare them, I argued.

Envision a round roast, perhaps. Or, perchance, for company, a delectable rump roast. Remember, I noted, everything from the neck down is rump. Of course, we'd have to figure out where the neck officially ends.

Drumsticks are out, I decided, but we'd have rib steaks and spareribs by the bushels.

Oh, there's just no end to it all.

Almost. Almost, I thumbed my nose at the hamburger and went flying to the nearest hillside in search of a tender morsel.

Almost. If hamburger goes up one more time . . .

Balancing the Budget
Unbalances the Mind

Although I couldn't think of many good reasons why we should adopt a new baby, there was one reason in particular which I was sure was not the one because of which we were doing such a thing.

(Now, while you're figuring that out, I'll proceed.)

The reason of which I am speaking is that we weren't rolling in wealth.

While Dirk has done extremely well in his particular field, radiologic technology, there is no fantastic amount of money in the work, and what with shoes and socks and underpants and milk money and car repairs, food and shelter and one thing and another, it seemed that paydays never came around often enough.

Like hundreds of thousands of other Americans, we were caught in the inflation pinch. In fact, our children thought Inflation was the name of the man who came to dinner.

I hadn't received a letter from the President yet, asking me to hold down on my spending, but I had read that he was making this request of all the big spenders in the country, so I assumed that he had just misplaced my address or something.

However, in keeping with the spirit of the request, I decided to do without a new car, a mink coat or any additional diamond necklaces.

I had decided early in the year to do without a vacation to Utah to visit the folks, but in view of the national economy (and our own), I revised my plans and decided not to vacation on the French Riviera instead.

I'll sacrifice anything for my country.

If inflation continued at its present rate, I was going to swear off a whole lot of other things too. Like food, shelter and clothing.

It really didn't appear the ideal time to add another hungry mouth to the household, but by again applying the Van Leer Theory, coupled with faith that eventually the country's money woes (and ours) would smooth over, we blundered onward, ever onward.

The whole blooming business of inflation and trying to make ends meet had, as a matter of fact, led me to the brink of an identity crisis.

In a day and age when everything is neatly diagnosed, labeled and pigeonholed in the proper spot, I couldn't decide where I fit into the scheme of things.

I consider it a shame, myself, that we humans are driven to categorize ourselves that way, but as Brian so succinctly put it one day, "Birds of a feather flop together."

My problem lay in trying to decide with which segment of society to flop. I even considered trying to flop independently, but that was against the rules.

When the provider got a raise, I cheered lustily because I thought we might then be promoted to upper middle class.

Then the house payment went up and oatmeal rose five cents per box, so we still had just as much trouble with too much being left over in the middle when we tried to make ends meet.

I was reasonably sure that we weren't either upper lower class or lower middle class, however, because the government hadn't come around to volunteer to help with the rent or to assist in buying groceries.

I hoped that there might be a middle middle class somewhere.

To further confuse the issue, I couldn't even decide what size I was.

I have always done most of my own sewing and hadn't given it a whole lot of thought, just proceeding along with a size ten pattern as I had done for years, when one day I was thumbing through the pattern book and chanced upon a table listing all the measurements for the various sizes.

I realized with a start that my particular measurements didn't fit into any one single size category.

My top measurement (not my head, you silly boy) was Junior Petite; my waist, Misses, and the other most commonly taped portion of the anatomy, Women's and Half Sizes.

I came away from the store in a state of deep depression.

I should have known better than to try something new in such a frame of mind, but I was determined that if I couldn't be some size, then the next best thing I could do, as busy mother of a large family, was to adopt a forward, young, modern outlook.

I decided to step up to pantyhose. Yes, I would shuck my girdle and go my way both sleek and unhampered.

Ha.

I stepped right up to the hosiery counter and looked over their stock. Then I bought a pair that said in big black letters: *Small. Fits Women 5-0 to 5-3.*

That's me—5-0. I took the pantyhose home, reveling in my new and modern approach to life.

I slipped into the bathroom and put them on.

After pulling them up to my armpits and securing them with a belt, I found they fell in graceful pleats down around my ankles.

"What you need," a friend assured me when I told her my tale of woe, "is Petite."

I trekked back to the store and got Petite.

Back in the bathroom, I slipped them onto my feet. Oh, bliss and things! They fit my legs so nicely—and hung on for dear life about halfway up my hips.

Possibly I could have gotten by with a pair of long suspenders, but I'd have lived in dread that someday the galluses would give and someone would be asking, "My, my. Whose hose?"

And what is there between Small and Petite, I ask?

I retrieved my girdle, gave up thoughts of going mod and went back to figuring out how to balance the budget, now that we'd decided to undertake that new mouth to feed.

We had saved $150 which would go to pay for the lawyer and for legal papers, etc., when and if the baby really did materialize. Beyond that, there was no promise of anything for the newcomer except an equal share in whatever we could afford, liberally salted with love.

It was in this atmosphere of cutting down some more that I thought of a way to save a few dollars.

I would cut Dirk's hair.

After all, my mother had trimmed up a husband and four sons for years. There couldn't be much to it.

We already had the clippers. When babies two and three had turned out to be boys, we had invested, not so much simply to cut hair as to cut the high cost of cutting. Dirk clipped the boys every not often enough, so if we could save another $2.50 every few weeks by having the lord and master also trimmed at home, why not?

I don't think Dirk was really convinced that it was the better part of wisdom, and after he was actually sitting on the stool with the clippers buzzing away and I gouged a chunk out of his neck on the first swipe, he got downright nasty.

However, I was determined and clipped away just the same.

"Keep telling yourself that this would cost you $2.50 at the barbershop." I encouraged him as the hair fell right and left.

"That's not much—considering," he muttered, spitting hair out of his mouth.

Undaunted, I clipped.

There was just this one little problem. I couldn't get the hairline to come out straight. Either I couldn't clip evenly or someone had put his ears on crooked.

Finally, however, I had it right—a perfectly straight line just above the tops of his ears. Not tapered, mind you, but straight. Keep in mind, for heaven's sake, that this was my very first job.

Then I cut his sideburns to match.

My biggest mistake was in letting him look into the mirror.

He didn't say a word—just went stomping out of the house, and I knew instinctively he was heading for the nearest barbershop.

Utterly ridiculous! I didn't see how any barber could improve on that haircut.

He couldn't. Dirk just had to be grim and bear it until it grew out again. (He didn't have to be so nasty. He could have spent a few weeks at a monastery, totally unnoticed.)

Never a word of gratitude, never a mention of the fact that I had saved him $2.50 and he was eternally grateful. Not one comment, kind or otherwise, that my haircut lasted him twice as long as any he ever had at the barbershop.

He never asked me to do it again, either. Much too hair-raising an experience, I guess.

Frozen Assets and Other Parts
of the Body

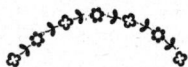

In Montana, winter always arrives with a thud.

No matter how long it fiddles around, wavering and feinting and pussyfooting and trying to pretend it's given up in favor of more Indian summer, one day it thuds and you know it's there to stay awhile.

No matter how you stomp up and down and kick your heels or bang your head against the wall, winter isn't going to go away until it darned well feels like it. You may just as well accept the fact with good grace.

I have trouble doing that.

Being a hothouse transplant from Utah, I fight it.

When the mercury starts playing Yo-Yo up and down the thermometer and finally takes the plunge down below zero, my spirits plunge right along with the mercury, and they stay in a state of frozen animation until spring thaw.

I have contended for years that the only smart people in Montana are the bears.

There they are, all snuggled up in their caves or hollow logs or what-have-you, wrapped in their fur coats and snoozing away the winter months each year.

In contrast, we supposedly more superior intellects shiver in the breezes, shovel mountains of drifted snow and slither and slide up the icy streets. We also blow on our fingertips and stomp our feet to keep from freezing on the spot.

However, this bear business does have certain drawbacks. I understand that when spring sprouts, the mama bears all bumble out of their caves with little bear cubs they didn't even know were there.

I don't think I could bear that, if you'll pardon the pun. As it is now, we can bearly manage the bear necessities. A cub-ble more would really cause what-fur. (To carry this nonsense just about as far as it can go without becoming entirely un-bearable.)

This particular winter was a real rouser. After a miserable autumn which one couldn't tell from winter itself without a score card, the real thing thudded onto the scene in late November with a crash that could be heard from Alaska to Idaho, and simply sat there.

In December the temperature plummeted down below zero and, despite my repeated incantations and daily prayers to the weather gods, stayed there for days on end.

Perhaps the weather gods did not recognize my muttered oaths and rantings and ravings as prayers. Perhaps I'm just not in very good standing with the weather gods.

I spent as much time as possible huddled in front of the furnace vent, making dire predictions as to how seldom I was going to write to the rest of the family when I finally was able to move to Honolulu.

The horribleness of the weather was compounded by the fact that it coincided with the children's Christmas vacation.

We skulked through the house bumping into each other and snarling. While ice crystals lent a certain sparkling clarity to the winter skies outside, tempers grew warmer and warmer inside.

Let me here admit that there is a certain beauty to be found in this weather. The houses all wore fluffy white shakos where the vapor from gas furnaces congealed, and the refinery down near the river was beplumed to beat old Ned.

After the first week of biting cold, we found to our utter amazement that we could actually go outside and function normally for short periods of time if we put on several layers of clothing and didn't stand still too long.

At least the children did. I still was content to sit in front of the furnace vent cursing the weather bureau.

One of the things you learned to avoid once outside, however, was touching anything metal with anything wet. You became mighty gingerly in the manner in which you took hold of a car handle, the trash can or anything else with bare hands.

Brian forgot once, though.

It was on one of those rare occasions when I was able to get in some furnace-sitting time. Laurel and Melinda were ice skating in the middle of the street. (The snow and ice couldn't melt so it just sat there. Each street had two sets of ruts, one coming, one going. You followed your set of ruts to the nearest intersection.)

Brian and Russell, bundled like onions, had trundled across the street to play with the neighbor children. Alan and Steve were engrossed with a model airplane they were putting together. Valerie was asleep.

It was indeed a rare moment.

And very short-lived. I had just settled down at my vent with the newspaper when Melinda came skating full tilt up the sidewalk screeching at the top of her lungs.

"Help! Help! Brian's tongue is frozen to the doorknob!"

I leaped up from the floor and ran to the door. Sure enough, Brian was on the neighbors' porch, firmly attached to their doorknob and bellowing in a strangled sort of way.

"'He's pulling his tongue off!" Melinda shrieked, announcing the glad tidings for all the neighborhood to hear. "He's bleeding to death!"

In my usual calm and efficient manner when faced with the little crises of childhood, I fell all apart.

I took a run at the door, remembered my bare feet and did an about-face.

"My shoes, my shoes," I roared, panic-stricken. "They were right here. Who's got my shoes?"

Alan and Steve, responding to the sounds of commotion, had bounded down the stairs and were standing there awe-struck at the sight of their mother screeching and darting through the house like a mad woman.

"Find my shoes! *Find my shoes!*" I screamed, while Melinda wailed at the top of her lungs.

I considered barreling across the street in my bare feet, but in view of the fact that the temperature was twenty-four degrees below zero, I reconsidered. It seemed enough that Brian's tongue was being quick-frozen, without my compounding the tragedy by bringing on a bona fide case of hoof *and* mouth disease.

Finally, on one of my passes past the kitchen sink, it occurred to me to fill a glass with warm water. I sent Melinda flying full skate ahead back across the street to pour water on her brother's tongue.

By that time, however, the neighbor had heard the cries of distress and had soaked Brian free with a wet, warm cloth. Bless her.

My son returned to the nest with his tongue hanging out of his mouth, thoroughly frostbitten and white. There was a nasty-looking gouge where he had tried to sever his relations with the doorknob by pulling.

I applied a cool, wet washcloth and made a quickie call to Daddy Van Leer at the hospital. He is the ultimate first-aid authority in the household in cases that don't clearly call for a doctor's care.

He told us to continue the washcloths and to give the little fellow an aspirin to alleviate the pain.

Gradually the chaos resolved itself. Brian finally fell asleep, with his washcloth hanging out of his mouth. The girls put their ice skates away and drifted downstairs to practice their piano lessons, the big boys went back to their model and Russ followed me into the kitchen, where I shakily cleared the lunch mess off the table.

"How come you didn't come and help Brian?" Russ accused me resentfully.

"I tried to, son. I really tried to, but I couldn't find my shoes."

"They're right in there, under my bed," he noted, in a tone that clearly indicated I was some kind of knucklehead not to have known that.

"How come they're under your bed? I remember now that I left them in the bathroom."

"I wore them after I took a bath because I couldn't find mine. I think you should have come to help Brian, anyhow." He went downstairs to provoke the girls into an argument.

Egad! I had failed as a mother again.

I wondered if I should have told him about my old recurring malady, freezaphobia.

I had been left with the disease, an intense fear of freezers and all things cold, after a harrowing experience as a young housewife.

I was defrosting our old refrigerator, an undertaking that's enough to make you sick all in itself, when it happened.

I was almost finished, but, from somewhere deep within, some hidden spring kept spewing drips into the freezer section so that I never got through mopping up.

In a moment of inspiration, I turned the control back on to freeze up the drips while I finished the job.

Let me give credit where credit is due. The control

worked so well that within seconds the top of the freezer was frozen and I was frozen to it. My hand, thoroughly doused in cleaning water, developed an immediate attachment to the roof of the refrigerator.

It was really a neat situation, because I had my right hand frozen to the far left corner of the machine and my bucket of cleaning water was at my far right on the cupboard.

After nearly strangling myself several times trying to reach the water, I got smart and hooked my left foot through the bucket handle, and by merely sloshing a half bucket of water up my pants leg and onto the floor, I was able to get the water within working distance of my free hand.

By flipping little handfuls of water upward for several hours (I'd *swear* it took that long) I was able eventually to thaw my paw off the beastly freezer.

The back of my hand was blistered from fingernails to wrist.

After an eternity or two, the skin all peeled off and the only aftereffect was the severe case of freezaphobia which I have already mentioned.

It was no doubt a subconscious recollection of my sad experience inside the refrigerator that kept me from rushing headlong into the winter chill to rescue Brian, thereby turning all ten toes into Popsicles in their shoeless state.

Try to explain that to a child, however. Freezaphobia they didn't understand. That I had failed as a mother, they understood.

Parenthood is hard.

There's a Lousy Mousy
in the Housy

A die-hard winter was staging a last-ditch battle for supremacy when the baby field mice came to live with us.

The back yard looked shabby in a slushed-up coat of halfhearted snow dumped there the night before by the waning season, and the sky overhead looked like the tail end of the dishwater.

But the breeze that whooped in and out of the corners, cutting into the piles of grimy snow, was laden with rumors of spring.

That's how it was on this March day when I noticed that there was more than the usual amount of activity in and out of the house for a school morning.

I finally nailed one of the boys and wrung a full confession from him, using the mild persuasion that if he didn't tell me what was going on immediately, I'd whop him one.

What he had to tell me was that there was a nest of baby field mice out in our back yard, hidden there the day before after the boys had made an early spring safari out onto the hillside.

They hadn't dared to bring them inside because we'd had

a few words recently about the amount of livestock that was finding its way into the house.

"Take them back to the mother right now," I demanded.

"We can't. The nest was in an old car up there and the mama mouse wasn't anywhere around. That's why we brought them home. They'll die if we put them back there, Mom. They'll freeze."

Torn. I was torn between the instinct that made me dread the thought of baby anythings wrested from their own mother and left out in our back yard in the cold—and my natural aversion to baby mice on the refrigerator.

As usual when I'm torn between the mother instinct and any other consideration, the maternal urgings won out.

In they came, two little creatures about the size of the end of my thumb, in a nest the little mama mousy had improvised of the cotton stuffing out of the car seat, no doubt.

The thing was crawling with teeny black insects, which I took to be lice.

Mice is one thing, but mice with lice are not nice. (I *know* that isn't grammatically correct, but it says what I want to say.)

We threw out the old nest and made a new one of clean cotton, put it in a box and set the whole thing up on the refrigerator.

The care and feeding of baby field mice, particularly those without their eyes even open yet, has never topped my repertoire of "Things I Do Well."

The kids had filled up the old lousy nest with bits of cold egg, toast, etc., from their breakfast goodies, but I felt certain that this was not the sort of thing upon which such wee beasties could best survive.

"Ha! They're babies, so they need milk," I deduced.

So while the youngsters trekked off to school, I found a medicine dropper and began dripping warm milk into those hungry little maws a drop at a time.

Somehow, it took most of the day.

Let me be honest. I had an ulterior motive in all of this. I kept hoping that when Daddy came home from work, he'd take one look, wrinkle his nose in disgust, say "Yick" and dispose of the little things, solving the problem while leaving my maternal conscience intact.

I should have known better.

When Father hove onto the scene, he assessed the situation, hemmed and hawed a little and then said, "Gee, I wonder if we could keep them alive."

Raising baby field mice had become (ta-ra-ta-ta-taaaaa) A Challenge.

As usual in this kind of situation, the children and Dirk were more interested in the idea of the challenge than in the dripping of milk and other fine points.

All night long I bounced in and out of bed like a Yo-Yo, dripping milk to beat old Ned. The little mice had an amazing capacity for such tiny creatures, and guzzled down a drop at a time with jolly good appetite.

As time went on, it began to appear as if we might be in the mice-raising business.

Then came an evening when I was busy with other things and Gerda undertook to feed the mice.

Bless her heart. With the gentleness she has always shown for all God's little furred and feathered creatures, she cuddled the little fellows and cooed to them while the milk heated up to the boiling point.

Then, without thinking to cool the milk, she pumped it in, still steaming hot.

Mousy Number One showed his displeasure by curling his tail and dying on the spot. The second one lived until the following afternoon. Both were buried with much pomp and ceremony in a little box under the kitchen window.

Once again it had been proved that Mother Nature cares for her own better than the Van Leers can.

We didn't have any little creatures of the wild for a whole week or so after that. Then I came home one day to find that a baby gopher had taken up residence in our bird cage.

That was all right, I suppose. The bird didn't need it any more. He had snacked on my Fiberglas curtains one day and died of indigestion.

I had learned my lesson, however. I washed my hands of the responsibility for any baby gophers and ignored it steadfastly, even though the bird cage was sitting on the kitchen cupboard and ignoring it was difficult to do when I needed space to cook or bake or any of the mundane things that mothers tend to do with kitchen space.

The gopher lasted for a couple of weeks, and then it was decided in solemn caucus that it was old enough to fend for itself and turned loose back in the fields.

I kept hoping that the adoption I was looking forward to so earnestly would be more successful than the others I had experienced so far that spring.

Don't Call Me Honey, Baby

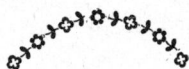

One day not long after the gopher had gone its merry way, I noticed something funny down in our basement.

It wasn't the fact that there were two salamanders running loose. I knew all about them already. The kids had turned them loose when I demanded, however unreasonably, that they be removed from my cake pan so that I could go back to cake baking.

(Eventually, the salamanders succumbed and I removed them, stiff and stark, by the tails from under the washer.)

No, that wasn't it.

What was so funny down in our basement was that there was honey leaking all over the place.

Let me begin at the beginning.

Sometimes we buy food in large quantities, because in large quantities is how we eat. That's how come we had two five-gallon cans of honey down in the basement to begin with.

And all had gone well up until now. However, it appeared that some little party had in the meantime pounded nails into one of the honey cans. (The little party responsible shall here go unnamed, because we could get no one to confess. Russell did suggest, however, that it may have been a burglar.)

Howbeit, the sticky stuff was oozing out of a number of nail holes and collecting in a puddle on the basement floor.

Realizing right away that something must be done, I decided to do something. I decided to transfer the honey from the leaky five-gallon can to a whole five-gallon plastic container.

And that's where the fun began.

To begin with, I couldn't move the can. Five gallons of honey weigh a heap—something like seventy-five pounds, I would judge from the way my back popped when I tried to lift it.

Dirk helped by getting the can upstairs to the kitchen. Then he made a big incision in the top so that I could scoop out the contents.

During the time it had sat in the basement, the honey had congealed, as honey is wont to do when left to sit for any length of time. I was in the habit of melting a small amount at a time to meet our needs.

After surveying the situation, I decided that scooping out the honey in its current congealed state would have taken somewhere in the neighborhood of fifteen years.

In an inspired moment, I set the can on a cooky sheet and, by dint of much effort, transferred it to the oven. Then I turned the heat up to "just barely" and went about my other work.

Oh, say, it worked just great.

The next time I looked, there were about three quarts of honey in the bottom of the oven and more piling up all the time, leaking out of the seam of the can.

Even in a state of shock, I was aware that the can had to come out of the oven. Mustering all my super-strength, I got a bear hug on the cooky sheet and heaved.

The cooky sheet with its load of dripping honey shot out of the oven, buckled, and suddenly all the honey that wasn't bubbling on the bottom of the oven was dripping down my front and seeping into my shoes.

With a superhuman effort, I heaved the load onto the cupboard and then made a flash decision.

I whipped off my slacks and stood there in my next-to-nothings with honey in my shoes, wondering what to do next.

What I did next was kick my shoes into the kitchen sink. Then I grabbed a pail of water and started in on the mess.

At this highly propitious moment, the children started arriving home from school for lunch.

"Look out for the honey!" I cried.

"What honey?" Laurel asked, plowing through the middle of the honey.

"What honey?" Melinda echoed, following her sister through the honey.

I dropped my honeyed mop rag into my honeyed mop water and buried my head in my arms.

That was a mistake, because while I wasn't looking, Brian came through the door.

"Look out for the honey," Laurel and Melinda screamed in duet.

"What honey?" Brian asked, plowing through the middle of the honey.

Thank goodness Alan and Steve didn't get home for another half hour, being elementary school upperclassmen.

I sat in the middle of my honey puddle and directed operations.

"Take off your shoes and then stay in the living room, all of you," I directed. *"Don't* come back in here."

At this juncture, Russell opened the basement door and walked through the honey. He'd been downstairs playing.

"Why can't the kids come in the kitchen?" he wanted to know.

"Look out for the honey!" we all screeched simultaneously, albeit too late.

"What honey?" he asked.

It served them right that they got peanut butter and honey sandwiches for lunch—served in the living room. It would have been a shame to waste all that perfectly good honey still seeping out of the can, as long as it was just sitting there anyhow.

I cleaned up their shoes and sent them back to school, and then in a short time (something like the first two million years of eternity) I had the mess all cleaned up, sticky wicket and all, as the English would say, I suppose.

Well, actually, we had a little sticky residue that hung around for weeks, so that every time you approached the general area where the honey had been (i.e., the entire kitchen, counting shoe prints, etc.), you were apt to stick a bit to whatever you touched.

Now that the residue has disappeared, however, I can recall the whole thing with a certain attitude of gratification, knowing that I have been where others may never go.

Not proud, but—you might say—a little stuck up.

You, Too, Can Enjoy the Flu

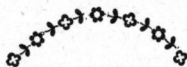

When March began cluttering up the calendar, I finally got some relief from the tension of waiting for word on our proposed adoption.

We didn't get any word, but what we did get was a full-scale epidemic of the flu all our very own, and I didn't have time to wonder if we were ever going to get that new baby. One by one, the youngsters collapsed in moaning miserable heaps on the living-room floor, until I had a wall-to-wall infirmary.

I wandered among the crew with an ice-cream bucket and a bottle of aspirin, trying to anticipate which one would throw up next. I think my batting average was down in the one hundred area.

When Dirk came home from work looking flushed and droopy-eyed, I ushered him into the west wing of the Van Leer Clinic for Flu-Bitten Indigents and provided him with his own personal ice-cream bucket and bottle of aspirin. Private patients have special privileges.

After several days and nights of Florence Nightingale-type service, I had a sudden inspiration.

No one has ever done anything to help people enjoy the flu. There's a book around on how-to-do everything else I can think of, but not one word on how to get the most enjoyment out of six kids and a husband all flat on their backs with the bug.

I could see my duty clear. I decided on a semi-factual, historical treatise entitled: "You, Too, Can Enjoy the Flu."

Pausing only long enough to clean up the carpet and to pass around the ice-cream bucket, I flung myself headlong into my work so as not to deprive humanity any longer.

Based on my long observation of flu-ridden folk (anything over fifteen minutes becomes long) I began outlining my masterpiece.

INTRODUCTION

It has always been my feeling that a mother should be able to enjoy the flu right along with her family. There is no reason why this should be a time for drudgery and complaining.

Remember, the family that is sick together will stick together.

Flu time should be a fun time, a time for togetherness. (If you won't all fit on the sofa, you can fit quite a few on a bed, lying crosswise.)

CHAPTER 1. WHEN TO HAVE THE FLU

It isn't wise to have the flu just any old time the notion strikes. It takes planning to get the full benefit of its effect.

For instance, try to avoid the disease when the house is all in order. If all the spare bedding is in the wash, the house in a mess and all the ironing stacked up to the ceiling, that's a good time.

Also, if you can be involved in some big project, such as painting the entire house, varnishing the floors or pickling cucumbers, it helps to take your mind off how sick everyone is.

CHAPTER 2. SYMPTOMS

Flu of the type we are discussing generally has two symptoms: "Frowing up" and "Dire rear." Both occur simultaneously among the sick members of the family.

If one person shouts, "Mama, I'm frowing up," let him.

If two persons shout, "Mama, I'm frowing up," and you are a two-bathroom family, toss a coin to see who goes upstairs.

If three or more persons shout, "Mama, I'm frowing up," you are perfectly justified in running to the nearest telephone and calling a realtor. Put the house up for immediate sale.

When frowing up and dire rear occur together, you certainly do have my sympathy.

CHAPTER 3. CARE AND FEEDING OF THE FLU-BITTEN

People with the flu have very sensitive appetites. You will find that one can abide nothing except pizza. Another can tolerate only chicken soup, while still another says that the only thing that appeals to his appetite is chop suey.

Still others want nothing. I suggest you feed them all the latter.

I should also mention here the matter of calling a doctor. When attempting to decide if the services of a medical expert are needed, in addition to the ice-cream bucket and the aspirin, you have two choices:

Call the doctor at the first droop of an eyelid and have him look down his nose at you for bothering him with trivia in the midst of the flu season, or wait until the patient is in need of intravenous feedings and have the doctor wonder why you didn't call him sooner. The choice is up to you.

There are a few hints I can pass along, based on years of childhood ills, that may help you in making a choice:

If the child has a runny nose, pink cheeks, an elevated temperature and a cough, it can definitely be said that he has one of these:

A. Measles
B. Chicken pox
C. Flu
D. Pneumonia
E. Whooping cough
F. Scarlet fever
G. Mumps
H. The Dreaded Mokus

However, don't fret about making an accurate diagnosis immediately, because you can be sure that, in any event, the illness is:

A. Serious
B. Not serious

CHAPTER 4. TAKE TIME FOR CRYING

Taking time out to feel sorry for yourself during a siege of the flu is essential. It's the only way a mother can really get her share of the kicks, especially if she's not feeling top-of-the-world herself.

Of course, just saying it is easy. Planning time for crying isn't all that simple. Certainly it can't be accomplished during the day with all that frowing up and dire rear going on. And it's one of the unwritten laws of childhood that the nicest time to be really sick is at night.

A child who merely moans during the day will run a raging fever and scream with vague and meandering pains at night. And if you're *both* going to cry, it gets kind of hectic.

If the mother really wants to get in some solitary crying

time, she must set the alarm clock for one half hour before the usual time that the family awakens.

At this time, all the sick ones automatically go to sleep. You may then retire to the basement and moan softly or cry right out loud with your head in a pillowcase. Or go outside and bay at the waning moon. I don't blame you.

CHAPTER 5. HOW TO KEEP FLU FROM SPREADING

Avoid contact with those who are ill as often as . . .

(I wasn't able to finish this chapter because I got the flu. Someday I'm going to get back to it, though, and I even have a thrilling sequel in mind: "Leprosy Can Be a Blast." Can't you just hardly wait?)

The Worm Turns My Stomach

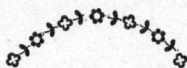

In many parts of the country, the robin is the harbinger of spring. Around here, it's the worms.

They don't pop out of the ground chirping, "Spring is here! Spring is here!" They just show up in the vegetable drawer of my refrigerator in little ice-cream cartons, signifying that spring and fishing time—synonymous in this area—have arrived.

I don't get too pushy about the situation as long as they stay in their little cartons, but on those occasions when I've discovered them mingling in the polite society of my lettuce and tomatoes, I've been inclined to say "Darn it!" Loudly.

The fishermen in the family don't always depend on cartoned crawlers, however. When time permits, the little boys spend a lot of time out digging among the petunias and bleeding heart, gathering in the harvest of night crawlers.

I don't mind that, either, as long as they remember to empty them out of their pants pockets before the pants go into the washing.

Russell in particular was entranced with worms this

spring-we-adopted-a-baby. After the ground became thawed enough, he and the little girl next door spent a lot of time digging, with an eye to raising the wiggly little beasts.

My tendency is to avoid any projects that deal with worms, and I might never have been aware of the depth of their undertaking had they not come to me for advice in the matter of separating the mama worms from the papa worms.

Russell was quite concerned with this aspect of it all, because we had told him recently that everything must have both a father and a mother.

Well, now. Try explaining for a four-year-old how come, if everything must have both a father and a mother, worms fall into a different category.

Go ahead and tell him that somehow, when the original plans were made, worms turned out to be asexual critters who don't pay any attention to the rules. Go ahead.

I took the easy way out.

I picked out the biggest, fattest worms, being careful all along to point but not touch, and proclaimed them the daddy worms.

Russell and his little lady friend seriously went about the job of pairing them up and housing each pair in a little box. Certainly if worms ever had ideal conditions and an abundance of tender loving care to create an atmosphere conducive to procreation, these did.

However, as time went by and the worms not only did not multiply in their little boxes but showed definite signs of shriveling up and dying, Russ decided Mom didn't know much about worms after all.

When the odor of putrefaction began filtering out from under the basement stairs where the worm colony had its abode, I issued an edict: "Out! Out! Out!"

Russell and Tania were all for giving the poor creatures another chance, but I felt they'd had chance a-plenty. We'd even given them the advantage of having a partner just in case, although heaven knows what one worm sees in another to engender love and respect.

Having been deprived of his worm-raising project, Russell was thrilled no end when the spring day arrived that Daddy proclaimed warm enough for the first family fishing fun of the year. Russ and Brian were assigned the task of rounding up some bait, and they disappeared with joyful whoops and hollers in the direction of my garden patch.

Before long they were back, mucky and exhilarated.

"How'd it go, kids?" I inquired, shuttling the potato salad into a box.

"Fine," Brian reported proudly. "We got thirty-two. They're out in the car."

"Great. Did you find a can big enough for that many?"

The long, thick silence which followed was fraught with meaning. We had (ta-ra-ta-ta-taaa) Problems.

"All right, you two," I said. "March, march, march."

I marched behind them out to the car and counted carefully as they retrieved bits of bait from under the seats, between the seats, on the seats and off the floor.

When we got up to thirty and it appeared that this was all we were going to find, I began making plans to call the whole thing off.

"Well," Russell commented helpfully, "maybe we didn't count right."

That's right, I told myself. Maybe they just didn't count right. Could be they actually had forty or more of the blooming things and everything in excess of thirty is still crawling around there in the car. I shuddered.

When Dirk came around checking to find why the picnic fixings weren't being packed, there was a lengthy conversation as to whether the duties of motherhood included riding in a worm-infested car.

Eventually all the children had gathered around to express an opinion, the general consensus of which was to the effect that Mama was sure being silly, and that if we didn't get going the day was going to be shot, for heaven's sake. I'd been outvoted again.

I reluctantly packed up the lunch goodies, sweatered and wrapped the baby and climbed into the car, keeping a careful watch where I stepped and sat.

To the observer, I'm sure it may appear ridiculous to be so fussy about the company one keeps. But if they want me to go fishing with them . . .

Actually, however, when I say I'm going fishing, I don't precisely mean that I'm going fishing.

What I do mean is that I'm going to sit at the edge of some lake, hopefully in the shade of a tree but likely in the blazing sun, "shagging" youngsters in and out of the water. Ditto their shoes and socks and underpants, the paper plates and cups and any odd bits of food that look as if they might float.

In between, I fulfill my duties as chief cook and bottle washer for the expedition.

This involves finding the most nearly level spot of ground within shouting distance of the water and then making several hundred trips back and forth from the car, toting the lunch under one arm and the baby under the other because there's no place to put her down.

I was just making about my ninety-ninth trip, with Valerie under one arm and the potato chips under the other, when I noticed something fantastic.

The real fishermen, Dirk and the two older boys, who had disappeared over the horizon a few minutes before trailing rods and reels, fishing line and lures, now reappeared over the horizon.

I waited with potato chips and Valerie under my arms to find out what quirk of fate was bringing them back in anything under four hours—their usual fishing session.

When they got close enough to see, I was able to determine right away that fate had really been quirked good this time.

It seems that on his very first cast, Alan had snagged something—the back of Steven's ear.

The hook was well embedded behind the ear, still complete with a marshmallow and a worm. (I've often felt this was a dirty bit of double-dealing, leading a poor fish to think he's getting a little goody, whereas what he's really going to get is a mouthful of worm.)

Well. Fishhooks being what they are, this particular one seemed destined to remain where it was. There was no hope of pulling it out because of the barbed end, and we had nothing with us with which we could cut the eye off the other end in order to push it through.

There wasn't much need for discussion. We simply teamed up and managed to get all the gear and children back in the car in about twenty-five trips and headed toward the nearest hospital emergency room some fifty miles back that-a-way.

As conversations go, there wasn't much going on the way back to town.

Steve sat between Dirk and me with the worm dangling down his right shoulder and the marshmallow snuggled up to his ear.

We all smiled a lot, but no one dared to laugh right out loud for fear Steve's feelings would be wounded beyond repair. When one has a fishhook in one's ear, one hardly feels it an occasion for levity.

In the emergency room, the nurses also managed to keep their mirth under control, at least when Steven was looking.

Doctor Bob, responding to our call for help, was not nearly so subtle. He hooted and hollered all the while he was snipping off the eye, pushing the hook on through the flesh and repairing the wound.

And why not? It was probably the only time in his career that he'd have an opportunity to excise a worm and a marshmallow in the same operation.

The day held one bright spot. With everyone carrying something, we had the car emptied in a mere ten trips or so, and our dinner was all ready for us.

And this was only the *first* of our family fishing fun for the year, I told myself.

I wished mightily that we'd get that new baby. That way, I'd have an excuse to pass up the next fun-filled excursion.

It Doesn't Add Up

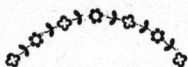

Life cannot all a bed of roses be. Nor all weekends.

After all that family fishing fun, it was a relief to get the school children back into school.

And it was not a moment too soon, either, for this was the week when I discovered an insidious plot to undermine the parents of America.

Laurie came home from school one afternoon loaded with homework and calmly announced: "You know what we learned today, Mama? A equals birds."

It was the New Math! I'd been aware for some time that the school was initiating New Math into its curriculum this year, and I'd scanned the papers the children brought home, totally ignorant of what it all meant.

But this was the first time I'd come face to face with New Math.

"A equals birds," Laurie continued, engrossed in her work, "but does B equal ice-cream cones or kittens?"

Ha! They can call it New Math all they want to, but suddenly I recognized it as a conspiracy to alienate children from their parents.

For years now, my Old Math students had been coming home, and caught in the toils of homework, they'd ask:

"Mom, what is six times nine?"

Quick as a wink, I'd have the answer.

"Fifty-four, dear."

Ah, the awed silence as I rose three notches in that grade schooler's estimation. Imagine anyone as ancient as Mom knowing that six times nine is fifty-four.

Now Laurie was sitting there wanting to know if B equals ice-cream cones or kittens.

I could have guessed, of course, but what good would there be in starting a charade I could not follow through for all of the years that modern math would be with us? Next thing you knew, one of them would want to know how many As in a fried chicken, and the truth would be out anyhow.

"I don't know," I admitted, feeling my image slipping something fierce. I could see gray days ahead.

The generation gap was on the verge of becoming an uncrossable crevasse. The cry had been, "Don't trust anyone over thirty." Now, no doubt, it would become, "Don't trust anyone who can add fifteen and fifteen and get thirty."

I brooded about it for days. I even considered going to school and learning New Math along with the youngsters. But with one new baby and another hoped for, I didn't have time, and besides, you can't teach an old dog new equations, can you?

It wouldn't do any good to talk with the teachers, either, I concluded. What would they care about a parent's battered image?

No doubt their attitude was that this modern math was just the ticket to prepare children for the crazy, mixed-up world into which they'd been bounced.

Maybe they're right, I conceded. But they'll never convince me that A equals birds. A may stand for Apple, but—equals birds? Never, never, never.

I considered a letter to the school board:

Dear Sirs:

As a taxpayer [*that* ought to set them back on their heels] I wonder if I might offer a suggestion.

While modern math is doubtless *the* thing as far as educators are concerned today, I can think of no compelling reason that my child needs to know that A equals birds. She may live out her lifetime without ever having any direct contact with birds, except those that flock out on our driveway to clean up the bread crumbs we put out there for them.

Even though my school children and I have spent countless pleasant hours deciphering the new system [*I'm* not going to be the one to hint that parents have become the laughingstock of the grade school set. Let them think we enjoy it], I am wondering if a more practical approach to mathematics might not serve the youngsters better in the long run.

There are a number of mathematical truths which, to my knowledge, have never been included in a textbook but which are common knowledge to every mother.

If you are interested, I would gladly volunteer to compile a number of them for inclusion in your curriculum. As a brief example, consider the following:

The number of times you yell, "Shut that door!" multiplied by five cents equals enough money to spend the winter in Bermuda. (In Montana, this includes tips.)

The number of times you send a child to the store for some little item and he returns with the little item you wanted is zero.

If you have eight apples and take away one, you then have none. (If one child discovers that another has an apple, there's nothing for it but to pass them all around, leaving only the empty bowl.)

Some parents feel that there is no way to divide things exactly equal so that there are no screams of discrimination with each serving.

Nonsense! While there is no precise mathematical equation to aid here, there are some fantastic new devices which measure things to within a millionth of an inch. It is probable that a family could obtain a good used model for twenty to thirty thousand dollars, so there's no use spending a lot of time in school learning about fractions.

Then there is the law of averages, which works slicker than a whistle most of the time but fails miserably every whack in the case of a five-year-old putting his shoes on the right feet. Don't count on it, either, to get the family through 50 per cent of its meals without having milk spilled on the table.

If the schools are going to do right by the students, which, of course, is the sole aim of those of you who are members of the school board, they should also teach something about the theory of relativity. I'm speaking of the relativity of what youngsters say, of course.

For instance, *"Every* other girl in our room has purple tights. I'm the *only* girl in the room without purple tights," being literally translated, means, "There's one girl in my class with purple tights and I think they're super."

Other examples:

"You always make *me* do everything." (You've asked him to do something.)

"You *never* let me do anything." (You won't let

him stay up until 1 *a.m.* to watch *The Mad Vampire of Mucky Swamp.*)

I could go on here with many, many other items that should be included in the teaching of mathematics, but realizing that your time is valuable, just let me emphasize that I stand ready to assist in a reorganization of the program at any time.

Feel free to call on me for advice.

Sincerely,
Twila Van Leer (Taxpayer)

Naturally the letter never got written, because, of the well-meaning projects I consider, the number I actually accomplish is about 50 per cent.

I decided I might as well learn to live with New Math, since I wasn't equal to a fight with the school board.

What a Beautiful Rotten Day

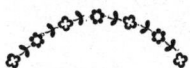

What a rotten day!

I just knew it was going to be *that* kind of day when I staggered out of bed with my eyes still at half-mast after flipping in and out of the sack while Valerie wailed the ancient music to welcome new teeth by.

My suspicions were confirmed when I yawned my way into the kitchen, where Russell was standing on a chair looking at three dozen eggs. The three dozen eggs were broken and sloshed from one end of the kitchen to the other. It was truly a sight to see.

Actually, that's an exaggeration. Oh, it was truly a sight to see, all right, but there weren't quite three dozen eggs on the floor. Only thirty.

They had begun the day in an egg tray delivered to us by a friend who lives in the country. The trays hold thirty. Russ had got tired of waiting for me to get out of bed and fix his breakfast, so he'd taken the tray from the refrigerator and prepared to make his own scrambled eggs.

There they were—scrambled all over the kitchen floor.

It was eggs-actly the kind of situation that makes me so

hard-boiled. I shelled out a spanking before I could stop to think: "Patience, Mother. Don't shoot until you can see the whites in their eyes."

Russ chickened out and scrambled away while I stood there like a dumb cluck, so bewildered by the mess that you could have knocked me over with a feather. This business of being a mother is not all it's cracked up to be, I concluded. Especially when the yolk's on Mom.

(Sorry about that. Sometimes I get started and just can't seem to quit.)

For a few minutes I considered leaving all thirty eggs right where they were and decorating around them. But they clashed terribly with the green shampoo Russ had used to paint the walls a few days before.

There was nothing for it but to lay into the job. There's no easy way to clean eggs off the floor, you know. I just started from scratch, and by the time I was through I was ready to fly the coop. (Oh dear, there I go again.)

Eventually the mess was pretty well cleared up and I turned the finishing touches over to the big girls because the morning was half shot and I was late.

What a rotten day!

What I was late for was parent-teacher conferences at the school. The administration planned these intimate little tête-à-têtes twice a year to allow the parents and teachers to brief themselves as to what the youngsters were up to and down in.

I can't speak for all parents, but I approached these sessions with fear and trembling. And all because of Show and Tell.

I can never be sure what has been shown and told. Which teacher knows which little tidbit about our private lives? And is it true?

For instance, how would you like to have your breast pump taken to school and explained in detail to a roomful of goggle-eyed first graders?

Melinda had shown just one grain of good sense in this

undertaking—she'd transported the pump to and from its moment of glory in Show and Tell in a plain brown wrapper.

I understood, too, that word had got around through the grade school grapevine about our new toilet seat. Included in this juicy bit was the news that Mama broke off the old one when she stood on it to reach into the medicine cabinet.

The new one is green, our Show and Teller explained, just to be sure everyone was filled in on all the details.

And now I must face these teachers eye to eye across a desk. Without doubt the greatest threat to the solidarity of the American family today is Show and Tell.

And I was late, a fact that would no doubt further endear me to the faculty at Riverview, not to mention the other parents whose conferences also would be thrown off schedule.

I left the girls joggling the baby and digging egg out from under the refrigerator and the little boys watching the big boys put together a model airplane and made a mad dash for the school.

Let me here say that I have nothing but admiration for the teachers in our school system. (Consider the alternatives. What if I had the children home all day every day all year? Heaven help me!)

We managed to get through all four conferences without any mention of Show and Tell. Possibly they felt that if they didn't dwell on Show and Tell, I could forget the things the children told me about what the teacher said in an irate moment.

In all, it was quite an agreeable morning, with nothing more earth-shattering reported than the fact that Brian had written his name in crayon on the floor in the kindergarten room and had had to stand in a corner.

While I was properly shocked and sympathetic, I could have countered with the information that Brian, since he learned to write his name, had put his signature in about twenty locations throughout the house that could have done without it. And if *that's* all the complaints they had . . .

Maybe it was only a semi-rotten day.

When I got home, the baby was still unbathed, the children unfed and mostly unclothed because the socks were all in the washing, which wasn't done, the kitchen was deep in cereal with which they'd fended off starvation, and Brian had painted his face and forehead with airplane glue.

Immediately I grabbed for Dr. Spock, and let me tell you, I was mighty disappointed when I found not a single word on how to remove airplane glue without also removing skin and, possibly, the eyesight.

I had to start calling doctors, and since this little event occurred, needless to say, during the lunch hour, there wasn't a doctor to be found. Finally I resorted to our friendly neighborhood pharmacist, who cautiously suggested that I try fingernail polish remover.

All this time, Brian stared at me without blinking. You see, it wasn't so much the fact that the glue had crinkled his skin and made his hair stand up like porcupine quills as the fact that he had glued his eyelashes to the top of his eyes and couldn't have blinked had he so desired.

Carefully, very carefully, I applied polish remover to a small test area near the hairline. When the skin relaxed and the hair flopped down over the hairline in a damp sort of way, I proceeded gingerly on down to the eyelashes.

In a few minutes, except for a little rosy color about the eye briars (his own description), he was blinking right along with the best of us. You might say he was a blinking mess.

What a rotten day!

That left only the washing, sweeping, bathing, lunching, dressing and general housecleaning for that day. And it was only about 2 P.M. I should be able to get through by midnight easily.

A couple of hours later I had the washing going, the children fed and dressed and the kitchen floor semi-decrumbed in a mad effort to come to terms with this rotten day, when the phone rang.

It was Dirk.

"Hi," he greeted me. "How'd you like to have a new baby?"

"Oh, sure. Why not?" (Sarcasm dripping with each word.)

"I mean really. They're going to have one available."

"You're kidding." (Caution dripping with each word.)

"Nope. Flanders called from the hospital up on the reservation. There's just one catch. This baby isn't born yet. It might turn out to be a boy."

"We'll take it! We'll take it!" (Overjoyedness dripping with each word.)

"Well, don't start folding diapers yet. The mother is an unwed teen-ager and she's been living in California. We'll have to pay her transportation back here. But if you're really interested, I'll call Flanders and tell him to start things rolling."

We were going to get a baby! We actually were going to get ourselves a little papoose!

What a lovely day! What an utterly beautiful lovely day!

Cleanliness Is Next to Impossible

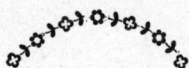

Our new baby wasn't due until the end of June, so I threw myself with a passion into the spring cleaning that I had been procrastinating over for three years, waiting for a convenient time.

Actually, I'd been waiting for just the right astrological moment. Each morning, I'd check my horoscope in the newspaper, and it was always telling me to put my financial affairs in order, or to look into that new venture that could result in big returns or to seek advice from bigwigs in charge. Never once did it say that I must throw myself into the spring cleaning I'd been putting off.

So, rather than antagonize the stars, I'd just gone along putting it off some more. No sense in tempting the fates, I figured.

Now, however, the time had come. The spots that traditionally collected odds and ends of this and that were in dire need of some rearranging, and there were some walls in the house that must either be painted or done away with completely.

Fortunately, when it comes to housekeeping, Efficiency is my middle name. Unfortunately, In is my first name.

Somehow, no matter how hard I try, when I'm finished it looks as if I'd gone through the house with an egg beater. With all the children running loose, I find it more profitable to spend my time trying to invent good logical reasons for not doing things.

This undertaking got a big boost when I went to a meeting with other ladies and during the course of the conversation one of them mentioned that she would *never* dry her dishes. Letting them drain in the fresh air was much more healthful, she noted.

Ever since, I'd spent my time racking my brains trying to figure out healthful reasons for bypassing some of my housekeeping chores.

The house had gotten pretty messy while I was doing all this thinking.

However, I did come up with several noteworthy time-savers, which I considered passing along to the National Association of Home Economists for their appraisal.

First of all, women shouldn't dust. A goodly amount of dust sitting around causes sneezing, clearing the nasal passages and expanding the lungs. Now, isn't that healthy?

Also, a little sticky stuff like soda pop or sugar left on the kitchen floor helps to prevent nasty falls. (Be sure that the sugar is spilled near the kitchen sink so that there will be ample opportunity for it to be mixed with water . . . even if you have to sweep it into the sink area from under the table. If you just have dry sugar sitting there and someone skids on it, don't say I didn't warn you.)

For heaven's sake, don't wax! Wouldn't you feel just terrible if someone took a dive on your freshly waxed floor and you had to go through life knowing that with just a little carefully planned carelessness it could have been avoided?

When you consider what some women spend for mud packs, you can see for yourself the utter futility of cleaning the bathtub. Why, after Brian and Russell get through bathing, I could get a head-to-toe beauty treatment absolutely free.

As for starching clothes, it's not only irritating to the skin, but downright sinful. You know what the Good Book says about stiff-necked people!

I worked and worked at trying to rationalize away the fingerprints on the woodwork, but the only thing I could come up with was this:

Suppose one of your children were kidnaped, but before paying the ransom, you wanted to be absolutely sure of the identity of the kidnapee. (Presupposing, of course, that you *wanted* the child back.) Matching the jam prints on the window sills with those of the victim would be your only chance.

That really wasn't too convincing, not even to me, and I wasn't hard to convince. So I turned my efforts to exhaustive research to find if the excessive amount of gamma rays coming in through clean windows might not be harmful.

It was at this juncture, however, that I found myself with one baby and another one imminent. So the world would have to wait with bated breath while I went on washing windows until my research could be completed.

Right now, I had work to do.

I began up in the attic, which contained several boxes of in-between sizes of clothing, my old tennis racket, which had needed restringing ever since the last time I used it when Alan was a baby, several bags of sewing scraps from which I intended to cut quilt blocks someday and an oddment of winter overshoes, some with partners, some without. Among other things.

I sat down on a box of odd-sizers to think it over. I really should begin by going through these clothes, getting the usable ones back into circulation and the unusable ones to the Salvation Army.

And that's just what I would do, but I wouldn't do it right now.

I wouldn't spend precious time now on that project. I'd just move the boxes down to the basement where they'd be handier and do them one at a time when there was more time available after my spring cleaning.

The tennis racket, on closer inspection, proved to be slightly warped. Quite a bit warped, actually. But if it were to be restrung, possibly the warping would be taken care of.

I'd put it down in the basement until I got time to get it to the sporting goods store.

We still needed quilts, so it would be a crying shame to get rid of the sewing scraps. In fact, there were a couple more bags in my sewing corner. I got them and set all of the bags at the attic door, ready to take down to the basement, where I'd be able to get to them when any spare moments presented themselves.

I've found from past experience that throwing away mismatched shoes or overshoes is a dreadful mistake. The mate always shows up within minutes of the garbage truck's departure. I put the overshoes into a box and set it by the door to take down to the basement, where I would sort them out, put the usable ones to use and find a spot for saving the odd ones in case the mates showed up.

Then I swept up the attic underneath all those boxes and looked around with a feeling of deep gratification. This spring cleaning was a snap!

I had Alan and Steve help me transfer the boxes and bags and tennis racket to the basement. But before we could store them there, I found there must needs be some cleaning out done in that vicinity also.

There were several boxes of books that hadn't been unpacked since our last move, a couple of Dirk's old Air Force uniforms, a big box with yarn lengths of varying degrees, a sack full of this and that that I had used for craft projects, including feathers, crepe paper, tissue, chenille strips, wire for stems, etc. Among other things.

Those books really needed going through and sorting. Some of them, if I recalled correctly, were school texts dating back to my elementary school days. But there was no point in trying to do that now with all this spring cleaning to do.

I'd just move the boxes up to the attic until I had some real browsing time.

I really debated over the uniforms. There was no chance in the world Dirk could have worn them now, in view of the fact that they had shrunk considerably around the stomach while hanging all these years. I had kept them with intentions of cutting them up to make trousers for the little boys. And the material was still perfectly good, so what I'd do is take them up to the attic until I could get to it. No sense in wasting good material.

That box of yarn was what really presented problems. I had found over the years that one of the unwritten laws of knitting and crocheting is that when you finish any item, you will run out of yarn with about ten stitches to go, so that you must buy a whole new skein of yarn. Hence you have always the big bulk of a skein left over, and since there's no point in wasting, you start another project with the leftover yarn, which runs out with about ten stitches to go, so that you must buy another skein of yarn, ad infinitum.

Anyhow, there was a lot of good yarn in there, most of it pretty tangled, but still good for things like afghans and slippers. If I put it up in the attic, I could spend a rainy day or two or three or a few weeks untangling it some day.

Ditto the crafts leftovers. Laurie and Lindy were always looking for something to make things with, and this little bag would be a veritable treasure trove for them. It could go up to the attic to make room for these other things, and on the first day that boredom set in, I'd whip it out and give them something constructive to do. If I could remember that I'd put it there. I recalled putting it down in the basement a couple of years before with the same thing in mind.

Alan and Steve grudgingly helped me back up to the attic with the books, uniforms, yarn and craft items, which I tucked into the corner recently vacated by the odd-sized clothing, the tennis racket, the quilt scraps and the over-shoes.

Back down in the basement, I swept up and put all those items where the books, uniforms, yarn and craft makings had been.

There, I sighed. All it takes to do a good job of spring cleaning is a little organization.

Now. On to the painting, and that would be a cinch. I'd seen it done on television many times. Some lovely young thing whips out a paint can, flips twice around a room the size of a formal ballroom while her husband naps, zaps everything back into place and stands there admiring her decorating job five minutes later with nary a hair out of place.

Hmmm. I wonder how they do that? I was wondering an hour or so later as I went through the house searching for the stick to stir the paint with. I'd set it down right next to the paint, then turned around for about two seconds.

I think the TV commercial just skipped the part where the lovely young thing chloroformed her children before she began the project.

Mostly, I decided as the days went by and the job continued, painting is a matter of keeping everything within reach . . . or at least where you can get to it before the children do.

I learned this the hard way when I took off all the switch plates and set them on a chair with the screws all neatly sorted out, then left them unguarded.

The next time I looked around, the screws were disappearing down the furnace vent one by one and the plates themselves were in serious danger.

At the time, I was spread-eagled with one foot on Valerie's crib and the other on the high chair, trying to reach the light fixture. I grabbed for Russ, forgetting that I had a paintbrush in one hand.

Oh well. What's a little paint on the face in his young life? At least I saved the switch plates.

Paint on the face paled into insignificance, in my esti-

mation, when I went to step off the high chair, realized
Melinda was playing jacks right underneath me, tried to
stop stepping and couldn't and fell onto the floor, spilling
about a quart of paint into my hip pocket, down my pants
and into my shoes.

Trying to keep everything within my reach and out of
the childrens' had some distinct disadvantages. I ended up
standing on the chair with a gallon of wall paint in one
hand, the quart of trim in the other hand, the paintbrush
between my teeth and the roller draped over my shoulder.

I could do everything except whistle, dance and paint.

Actually, I didn't mind the kids touching up in the room
where I was painting, but I did get a little miffed when
Brian took the brush out of the can and cleaned off the
avocado-colored paint on my apricot-colored living-room
walls. (I never can decide whether to paint my walls with
these exotic paints or to eat them.)

In spite of it all, eventually I was through, and I stood
back with the dripping roller to admire my new gold living
room.

"Gee, Mom. That really looks neat," commented Brian,
stroking the newly finished wall. Unfortunately, his
stroking hand was full of damp licorice.

Nuts! I'd rather make TV commercials. Chloroforming
the children first, of course.

A Rose Is a Rose Is a Weed
in My Book

With the inside of the house all slicked up, I was ready to take on the whole outdoors. Well, our own yard at least.

I'm not the world's best gardener. My green thumb has always been a little jaded, if you'll pardon the pun.

I love flowers just as well as the next man (unless, of course, the next man happens to be a botanist or a florist), but there's something about me that when plants get a close look, they just shrivel up and die.

Consequently, I've been content to let Dirk take care of the exterior decorating around the house. He has the Dutchman's touch when it comes to green things—inherited, no doubt, from his Dutch daddy.

Opa (that's Dutch for Grandpa) would never even twitch a leaf from a plant, no matter how far gone it might be.

"Let it fall off by itself," he insisted. "How would you like it if someone pulled off your leg when it wasn't really dead yet?"

Horrors! I can't even say that I'm wild about the idea of them taking off my leg if it were dead.

"Plants have feelings, too, you know," Opa proclaimed.

All of this in Dutch, of course. Opa came to the United States late in life and never did learn to speak any English.

But there was nothing lost in the translation. Although Opa has since passed on, I never can bring myself to twitch any leaves, and I am even loath to pluck up weeds, imagining that I hear heart-rending cries with each pluck.

As a matter of fact, and at the risk of offending garden enthusiasts from Kokomo to Saskatoon, I'd like to ask: What's wrong with weeds anyhow?

It's a shame how they've been maligned all these years. Who is it that decides what's a weed, anyway? You can't even tell them from the other plants without a score card.

In fact, some nitwits have been known to pull up every pansy in the place in their zeal to rid the garden patch of weeds.

I noticed this right away that spring when Dirk came in the house roaring, "Who's the nitwit that pulled up all the pansies?"

"You mean all those weeds?" I asked weakly.

"Pansies! Pansies, dear! You pulled every one of the pansies I planted." He appeared to be a bit upset.

"Well, I'm sorry," I apologized, "but why should the pansies have any rights and privileges over plants that look so much the same that your average, run-of-the-mill nitwit can't tell the difference?"

"Great Scott, woman!" he moaned, waving his trowel around like a maniac. "There's a difference. Flowers are flowers and weeds are weeds."

"How come?" I defended myself. "If you were perfectly honest, you'd admit that dandelions, morning-glories, crab grass and pigweed have a certain beauty of their own, when looked at with an unprejudiced eye."

He looked as if he might cry.

"I can't see any reason to go on coaxing the 'acceptable' plants, which won't grow for me on any terms, when there are dandelions and morning-glories just sitting around waiting for a chance," I went on.

"Ah well," he sighed, heading for the front yard, "at least the petunias are still with us."

I always planted petunias because one of my neighbors had told me a few years back that they were "the idiot's delight. They'll grow for anyone."

I thought it was very reassuring, because the first year I could claim almost without fear of contradiction that I was no idiot. Of the twenty-four plants I planted, only two produced blooms.

After that, Dirk took over. I planted, he watered, cultivated, fertilized and babied, and we always had plenty of petunias.

I felt so bad about the pansies, however, that I chugged out to the nursery to buy a couple more flats, albeit muttering, "Up with weeds! Up with weeds!" under my breath.

When I got home with them, I offered to replant them, but Dirk waved me off with some select comments that led me to believe I had been banished forever from the precincts of the flower beds.

Probably just as well anyhow.

Within a few weeks, with Dirk giving them plenty of tender loving care and manure and myself giving them a wide berth, we had petunias and pansies frolicking about in the spring sunshine in gay profusion.

And that lasted for about one day. Then Russ discovered them, and in the goodness of his little heart he gathered his mama a gay bouquet. They did better in gay profusion.

The bouquet lacked enough stem per flower even to stand up in a shallow vase. I floated them around in a bowl, at the same time explaining to Russell that he must never, never, *never* pluck up his father's flowers. And if he did, to get enough stem on them to put in a vase. But mostly, *never* to do it.

He nodded his agreement and vowed a solemn vow never to pluck a blossom from his father's garden patch again. He meant it, too. I watched him as he went back to his play, and he made a fifteen-foot detour around the garden patch.

Chalk one up for me. I'd really gotten through to him.

Ten minutes later, Russell was back in the house with another bouquet and the stems were plenty long. They'd been pulled up by the roots.

"Son!" I screeched, "you said you wouldn't pick any more of your daddy's flowers."

"I didn't," Russ explained patiently. "These are Mrs. Wolverton's."

A quick glance across the street proved that he was right.

"Let's put it this way." I sighed, pulling the drapes and preparing not to answer the telephone. "You pick one more plant without someone's specific permission and I'll plant you. In bed. Permanently."

I believe in calling a spade a spade.

Spooning It Out Isn't My Cup of Pablum

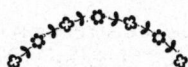

I would hate to leave anyone with the impression that I approached the thought of rearing two babies simultaneously without qualms.

I was the qualmiest. (My husband says that should be spelled with a capital B, but then what could an old Dutchman know about spelling?)

For instance, whenever I thought of having to feed two babies, I broke out in qualms just like some people break out in hives.

It is my contention that it was never intended that babies be fed. If the Good Lord had meant that we feed babies, He'd have provided some reasonably simple way to do it.

I don't mean milk. That's pretty easily accomplished one way or another. I mean solid foods—and whoever decided to call them solids has never had a lapful.

In the first place, the basic design is all wrong. Babies have far too many hands and mothers far too few. The mere sight of a spoon sets all the baby's arms in motion like a windmill, and the mother must wait for an opportune moment to whip the spoon through an opening and into the baby's mouth.

An opportune moment occurs each two thousand revolutions of the arms, or never, whichever comes sooner.

Until the infant is big enough to sit in a high chair, the feeder must prop feedee on her lap in such a way that both of feeder's hands are free, one to hold the dish, the other, the spoon. Any other appendages she can muster may be used to control those of the baby so that feeding may proceed.

I'd like to recommend that Mother lay the infant across her left leg, then put her own right leg across the baby's chest, being sure that all the arms are pinned neatly underneath.

I'd like to, but I'm afraid of what it might do to my standing with the local Humane Society.

Someone once suggested that I set the child on my lap with his/her right arm and shoulder tucked beneath my left arm, with my left hand around his/her shoulder and holding his/her right hand.

Once I figured out what she meant, I found it was nice, except that it put Baby's legs within firing distance and didn't really cut down on the amount of baby food flipped around the kitchen.

Well, you solve that one the best you can while I move on to the next point.

There isn't any convenient time to feed the little rascals, you know.

Invariably they sound their clarion call while you're in the middle of some time-consuming job that you can't leave without ruining something. Like stirring pudding or replacing the drapes or something like that.

So you hurry like the dickens, slopping through the job and making a mess of it. Then you run to the kitchen and heat up some baby food, all to the tune of that poor infant starving to death.

Then you make a mad dash to the cribside, armed with a tasty tidbit, only to find that the wee one has indeed died of starvation (after all, he/she hasn't had a bite to eat in two hours) or else gone back to sleep.

Unless you're *awfully* slow, it's always the latter.

Rather than have all that warmed-up food go to waste, you attempt to feed the little nipper while he naps. This results in the napping nipper napping with a chinful of food and utter frustration for the soup scooper.

Not to worry. Not to worry.

Just set the food aside and rest assured that as soon as it has cooled too much to be fed to the baby, he'll awaken screaming.

You feel free to go ahead and get involved in another project that will have to be interrupted when the screaming begins.

Assuming that the warmed-up food and the baby actually do get together eventually, the real fun begins.

Take a small spoonful of food and insert it well into the baby's mouth (providing you have managed to avoid all those hands and feet en route so that there is still food on the spoon).

Scrape the sides of the mouth and the chin with the spoon. Put the food back into the mouth. Scrape the sides of the mouth and the chin.

Etc., etc., etc.

After you have repeated this process about thirty times, you will find that you have scraped up and wiped away with a bib approximately three pints of baby food.

And that takes care of the first mouthful.

Just keep on with this spooning, scraping and wiping-up procedure and eventually the food will disappear.

Well, actually it doesn't disappear. You will find it all, plus interest, on the walls and furniture and any clothing within a ten-foot radius—farther if the baby chances to sneeze during the transferral from mouth to tummy.

Sneezing in babies is rarely a sign of a cold. Much more often it is an indication that he/she is being fed some colorful food such as spinach, carrots or beets.

Sneezing often occurs during an intimate moment when the mother is leaning close, cooing and cajoling a tasty tidbit into her toothless tad.

Looking at the world through rose-colored glasses is one thing. Staring at it through beet-speckled glasses is another kettle of fish entirely.

It occurs to me that in a country which has developed its technology to the point where it can produce the world's most repulsive TV fare and electric chin massagers, there should be someone who could invent a fuss-free food-feeder for babies.

The way I see it, it wouldn't take much to whip up a little apparatus with a suction cup on one end, to attach to the baby's face, and a hypodermic action at the other end, separated by a long plastic tube. That way, Mother could sit in another room, say the living room, and shoot the food into Junior's mouth long distance, while at the same time enjoying a good book.

Or how about a nice plastic box (with self-cleaning walls, preferably) similar to those used by hospitals for premature babies? It could be equipped with a vise to hold the baby's head still, and a super-sized eye dropper poised directly over the mouth.

It would have to have some sort of device to pinch the baby's cheeks so the mouth would remain open, like a little birdie's, waiting for Mommy to squirt the squirter.

Or, perhaps, a larger box, for Mommy herself, with only a couple of rubber-edged holes for the hands to go through in order to wield a spoon. Soundproof, maybe.

No, no. On second thought, not soundproof. Mother might never come out to feed the other children.

Well, anyhow.

I thought of these things as I fed Valerie, dodging the

drips and wondering what it would be like to do this for two infants.

And you *do* have to feed them, you know, so that they'll get big and strong and ready for potty training.

But that's a whole new chapter.

Potty Tinkles Ring a Bell

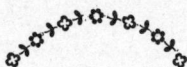

Over the years, I've done a great deal of bathtub sitting.

I'm probably the world's champeen bathtub sitter by now.

I don't sit *in* the bathtub. Specifically, I sit *on* the bathtub. On the edge.

I sit there to aid and abet, encourage, cajole, threaten and praise. I also make appropriate noises and go through all sorts of degrading explanations. In addition, I wipe up the puddles as we go through the periodic ordeal of (oh, joy and juleps) Potty Training.

If there had been some proper thought given to the problem in the beginning, children could be born with a few of the social amenities. But as things stand, there's no avoiding the issue. Eventually, the parent must take up bathtub sitting. Either that or plan on packing diapers in the school lunches.

Frankly, I don't mind too much until we get to that depressing state where the child has a general notion of what it is all about but fails to comprehend the scoring system.

To their way of thinking, a puddle somewhere in the general vicinity of the potty should count for something.

It must be a mystery to their little minds that the same parent who goes into ecstasies of joy over a puddle in the pot becomes a raving maniac over a puddle that just missed by inches.

One of the ruses parents use is appealing to the child's vanity in the matter of panties vs. diapers. My children have delighted in wearing the panties, but most often insist on putting them on themselves. As a result, they lope around practically full time with both legs through one hole and a little bare bottom trailing along behind.

Even when I put them on, they're generally at half mast. How come no one ever thought to put a belt on training panties? Or suspenders, for heaven's sake.

But to get back to the technicalities of potty training—

When you reach this stage in the child's development, you must decide whether you are going to give it to the child straight, calling a potty a potty, or clutter up the vernacular with silly terms.

I'm for giving it to him straight. A child who has learned the correct technical terms, such as "tinkle" and "potty," won't be so inclined to pick up corruptions later in the sandbox or the pool hall.

Now. Just suppose that you are able, in fact, to accomplish this undertaking and that the child does, indeed, learn to tinkle in the potty.

Then is the parent overjoyed and thrilled to the nub, so to speak?

Nay, not so.

As soon as the taddies have learned this wonderful art, they use it as a tool to torture parents unmercifully.

Take them out somewhere—anywhere—and immediately they begin to pipe the tune you've taught them: "Potty, Mama. Potty."

How it resounds and echoes—through the corridors of the local market place, rebounding from the pork and beans and caroming off the pickled beets; up and down the hallways of the school where you are attending Family Night for the PTA; careening off the pews in church where heads are bowed in prayer. Oh, blimy!

Parent is then faced with a dilemma. Is the child really in need, or is this just an excuse to create a diversion? Take a chance if you want to. I've learned the damp way to take them at their word (making many dry runs along the way).

Training they call it. Hah! With this kind of training I could get to be the world's champeen at the fifty-yard dash . . . the equivalent distance to the nearest potty from wherever you happen to be when the call is sounded. Unfortunately the child is set only for a forty-yard dash.

But until someone invents a child that comes equipped with some common sense, parents are stuck with the problem, so as mothers say from Arkansas to Zanzibar, "Bottoms up."

Those who feel that the training is all through when the potty is mastered have sure got a surprise coming, too. Hah! At this point, the child's training has only just begun—and if that's redundant, I meant every word of it.

Unless you want to be accused, and justly so, of rearing a houseful of slobs, you must train them to pick up behind themselves and to put away and to practice some of the social graces.

It would be much simpler to stand still and take the accusations, believe me.

If you want to know the satisfaction of any success at all in training children, you must be careful in your selection of those areas in which you desire them to be trained.

For instance, when Melinda was small, I decided to train her to dance on the kitchen table. I decided this after several swats on the diaper had failed to convince her that she must stay down from the table.

Obviously I was taking the wrong tack. Why *not* train her to dance on the table, if that was her natural inclination? Someday she might make a living doing table dances, and she could recall with tenderness that she got her start on her own kitchen table.

And then take the matter of coat hooks. I've trained every child in this family to miss those hooks by margins that you wouldn't believe. There isn't a one of them who can't toss a coat and miss that hook by a hair's breadth every time.

If they ever have a hook-missing event in the Olympics, we've got it all sewed up, and all due to early training.

They have also been known to miss the clothes hamper (a large one) with a bath towel 100 per cent of the time.

As they approach young manhood or womanhood, however, it is time for some really serious coaching in their relationships toward others.

I had occasion to give Alan a few pointers as to how a gentleman treats a lady when we went to the hospital one evening to pick up a neighbor who needed a ride home.

As we pulled up to the hospital door, I instructed Alan to open the car door for the lady friend, then shut it when she was safely inside.

My, he did do it beautifully. And she was so impressed with all this gallantry that she made the mistake of mentioning it right out loud.

"Yeah," came this little voice from the back seat. "My mother made me do that."

Begorra! I'd rather train porpoises.

Thmile When You Thay That, Mithter

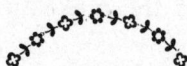

❀❀❀❀❀❀

Hey! Want to hear a story with real teeth in it?

Well, actually this is a story with false teeth in it.

Having made use of "falsies" for some years, due to a losing battle with pyorrhea, I've experienced several toothsome experiences, but this particular event took place on an ordinary-ish sort of spring day.

Laurel and Melinda were loping up the hallway with Russell sitting on a seat they'd made by grasping each other's arms. They were singing:

> For he's a jolly gorilla,
> For he's a jolly gorilla,
> For he's a jolly gorilla,
> Which nobody can be nice.

Brian was loping along behind them, waiting for his turn to be the jolly gorilla.

Alan and Steve were both at the table, finishing up homework that should have been done the night before.

And Valerie was in bed, afflicted with an untidy didy. And therein was my downfall.

I had been en route to the bathroom, teeth in hand (don't knock it; it's better than foot in mouth), when my motherly conscience convinced me that Val's condition should take priority over toothbrushing.

I set my porcelain pearlies on the kitchen cupboard and plodded on to the bedroom to alleviate the cribside crisis, waving the older children off to school as I went.

All might have gone well had I been able to get back to the kitchen before the milkman arrived.

Can you picture it? I in the bedroom, my teeth on the kitchen cupboard and the milkman leaning on the stove, waiting to be paid?

Russ had left off being a jolly gorilla and was finishing up his oatmeal, so I called him into the bedroom and in hushed tones asked him to please go in the kitchen and retrieve my cutlery from the cupboard.

He went dutifully into the kitchen, spent two jiffies searching diligently, then screamed: "Mama, your teeth aren't in here!"

Even then the situation might have been salvaged had not the milkman got into the picture.

"Sure they are," he pointed out to my little fellow. "They're right there on the cupboard."

I walked into the kitchen, retrieved the choppers, paid the milkman and refrained from beating Russell to death. And that's pretty good for a day when I was feeling pretty "down in the mouth."

It was a pretty sad way to start a day. What I really needed after all that was something to give my spirits a lift.

I didn't get it when Brian came home from kindergarten and dropped the morning's pile of paper work in my lap.

"See this?" he pointed out. "It's a picture of our family."

"Oh, I can tell that," I said.

It looked like a field full of scarecrows—just a whole bunch of stick figures with long fingers and naked as jay birds. Except for one fine specimen which stood in the center, three times as tall as the others and with lovely blue pants (fastened up around the neck, true, but pants, nevertheless).

"Who's this, son?" I asked, preparing to be modest. ("You mean that important one there in the middle with the lovely blue slacks is your mother? Oh, you shouldn't have.")

"That's Dad," my artist replied, with a look that clearly intimated that I had asked a ridiculous question.

"Oh."

It had just been brought home to me again. Motherhood is a futile undertaking—a thankless task.

Who goes through the process of bringing the offspring into the world to begin with, being left at the end with an abdomen that resembles a king-sized prune?

Mama does.

Who struggles through the trying months when in order to execute a didy change it is necessary first to wrestle the squirmy infant to the floor, plant a knee firmly on the chest and then dodge the flying pins?

Mama does.

Who is it that day in and day out feeds, cleans, nurtures, teaches, nurses, Band-Aids, scours and scrapes, chauffeurs, doses and defends the little dears?

Mama.

And who, in the wee hours before cock's crow, trundles the floor, stumbling over the day's accumulation of shucked-off toys, bleary-eyed and chanting the ancient chant to Make Teeth Come Through Quicker and Less Painfully?

Oh, by golly, Mama do.

And then, when the cherub reaches the age when its vocal chords begin to search for expression and the first word falls from its lips, would you care to guess what that word might be?

Dada. (Or just Da for the less articulate. But the meaning is just as clear. The child prefers his da.)

And when the pictures of the family come home from kindergarten, who is the central figure, the God-man, the hero, the scarecrow with pants? The da.

I decided I wouldn't make cupcakes for Brian to take to school for his birthday.

If there's a reincarnation, I speak to come back as a father-type.

Of course, with my luck, I'd come back as a father sea horse. I understand that they do all the producing, feeding, cleaning, nurturing, teaching, nursing, scraping, Band-Aiding, scouring, chauffeuring, dosing and defending of their species.

Yes, it's thankless, thankless, thankless. Only a fool would volunteer for extra duty.

Big Wigs Make a
Hair-Raising Tale

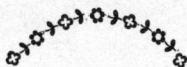

The more I thought about Brian picturing me as a scarecrow, the more depressed I became.

Maybe he did that because that's what I look like to him, I thought.

Bejabbers!

I looked at myself closely in the mirror. Hmmmm. Possibly to a little boy with an unsteady crayon finger . . .

By now I had developed a full-scale case of the quolly-bobbles, a rare affliction suffered by women who are rapidly approaching middle age a lot faster than they were a few days ago, who are the mother of eight-going-on-nine children and whose existence is drab, drab, drab.

One of the side effects of the malady is an appearance slightly tinged by scarecrow-edness which is most apparent to five-year-olds.

What I needed was a new head of hair.

Some women who suffer from the quolly-bobbles can be cured by the purchase of a new hat. I never wear hats, so that was the wrong remedy for me.

A deep-seated case such as mine needed something much more drastic, I concluded. I would give myself a whole new look, starting with a wig.

And *that* was drastic, let me tell you, because I've never really cared for wigs. I seem somehow to have been born into the wrong century, but I can't help it. I just don't care for wigs.

If ever there was anyone who should have been delighted when wigs became the *in* thing, it should have been I. I mean, I have this hair of my own that just sits there on top of my head doing absolutely nothing. (A bit like a scarecrow, if you know what I mean.)

About a year before Valerie was born, I finally had succumbed to the march of progress to the degree that I bought myself a wiglet. It sat atop my own do-nothing hair doing all sorts of exotic things—curling this way and that and all.

Everything went well, except that I suffered from a vague feeling that I was being false to those who looked at me and suspected that all that glamour was the real me. I knew better. I knew that up there underneath those divine curls was the real me—just sitting there doing absolutely nothing.

Well, when friend husband and I took a quick trip to Utah to visit the home folks, I took the wiglet along to amaze everyone and to fool the friends and relatives into thinking that Montana had done something wonderful for me.

"Would you look at that?" I could feel them thinking. "Why, even her hair looks better."

My charade might have gone off without a hitch had we not gone boating during a reunion with Dirk's family.

Whipping across the lake with the spray in my eyes and the wind whistling through whosever hair I was wearing, feeling exuberant and lightheaded, I suddenly realized why I was feeling so lightheaded.

There behind, sloshing along in the wake of the boat, was my wiglet. It resembled nothing more than a sopped-up Pekingese about to go under for the third time.

We turned the craft around and fished my hairdo out of the drink, and I rode back to shore with it draped around one finger drying out. My own hair just sat there doing less than usual.

I swore off wigs forever and ever.

But that was before I got the quolly-bobbles. Forever be hanged. In my present desperate situation I was ready to consider anything. So I did.

After considering for a few minutes, I went out and got a wig.

And oh my, oh my. Was I ever lovely. Scarecrowedness flew out the window and my drab life became fraught with glamour and excitement. I was the "After" in the Before and After ads. Feminine mystique hung about me like a bath towel. An aura of loveliness wafted fore and aft when I chanced to pass. Egad! It was marvy.

Then one day, all fraught, mystiqued and auraed, I hied myself to the corner grocery to buy baloney and oranges for lunch.

Now, there's one thing about Montana—at least the area where we live . . . (Actually, there are several things about it, but that way lies madness. Let us consider them one at a time and only after a good meal.)

The thing that I have in mind is the wind. You may have heard of it in songs referred to as "gentle breezes" or "whispering breezes." Well, maybe so. But the last "gentle breeze" I had anything to do with around here rolled me over three times and left me draped around a telephone pole.

And on this day when I went in search of baloney and oranges, it was whispering around at about ninety knots. (At sea they are referred to as knots because they tend to leave the sails all tied up. After a ninety-knotter, it takes the sailors days to get the kinks out. And you thought I didn't know anything about sailing. Ha.)

Be that as it may, I hurried through the store and gathered up the necessary items and a number of others and headed out the door with a big bag under each arm.

I was greeted by a hearty gust which lifted my lid and deposited it some thirty feet over that-a-way. I went running after my errant hair and stomped my foot down on it to keep it from blowing any farther.

There I stood, my arms full of groceries, my foot full of fur and the cape on my coat blown up over my head, covering up the mess that the wig was supposed to be remedying.

So I leaned over to snag the wig before it went wandering again, and dumped my oranges. They rolled merrily hither and thither around the parking lot.

All of the lunch-time crowd snacking at the snack bar in the store gathered around to peer out the window and laugh themselves silly.

Eventually I concluded that the only thing to do was to make a dash for the car and relieve myself of the groceries, letting the wind take my hair wheresoever it listeth. I hoped it wouldn't list to take it under the big truck that was delivering dairy products.

After I'd chucked the groceries, I returned to the chase. The jolly crowd of onlookers was only too happy to point out my wig for me. It was nestled up against the tire of a car and I snatched it up, retrieved my oranges and bowed to my audience. It was the least I could do after a floor show of that caliber. Some people have the most peculiar sense of humor!

Back home with my done-in hairdo, I called my friend Kerma to solicit some sympathy.

"Ha! You think that's bad?" she snorted. "Listen, I wore my wig to church a few weeks ago and when we knelt down for Communion, Jim was sitting behind me. When we stood up again, he knocked the whole thing off."

"Blimy!" I said. "What did you do?"

"Followed my first inclination," she confessed. "I swore at him."

In the weeks that followed, I soon found that there is a fierce type of one-upmanship in the area of wigs. Everyone who wears one has lost it at one time or another, it seems.

For instance, there was my friend who went to a movie with a plush wig hiding a welter of bobby pins. When they left the movie, the lady behind was wearing the wig on her coat button and friend was wearing the bobby pins.

Then there was the lady who attended a social affair at the church. Whilst she made conversation with others in the crowd, the infant perched in the arms of its father directly behind her made off with her hairdo. Since the father was looking in the other direction, he didn't realize the little fellow had filched her fur, and he wandered off. It was some time before the mortified lady was reunited with her toupee.

After hearing all these wild stories, and still smarting from my own sad experience, I swore off again. No wigs. Ever, ever, forever.

For me, the feminine mystique is a mistake.

Oh, Say Can You See?

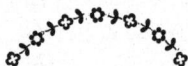

One of the things that happened during this spring when we were waiting for a new baby was that Alan turned twelve. That wasn't too surprising, because just the year before he had turned eleven.

However, it was rather a special birthday, because it marked his advancement from the Guide Patrol into the really-truly Boy Scouts of America.

We've always been rather impressed with the scouting program. After all, being trustworthy, loyal, helpful, friendly, courteous, kind, obedient, cheerful, thrifty, brave, clean and reverent is a pretty keen way to be. And we need all the help we can get.

Besides, it gives someone else the opportunity to spend time in the wilds with the fellers, and I'm all for passing the opportunity around every chance that comes along.

In addition, the Boy Scouts is one of the organizations that still foster the ideals of American living.

I realize that these days it's gauche to wave a flag, but at the risk of appearing corny, may I say I rather enjoy living in America.

Of course there are things that are wrong with the country, but I'm of the opinion that many of the things that are wrong are wrong because so many people abuse the things that are right.

No matter what's wrong with America, however, it's still one of the places in this world that you needn't amble out into the chill of night or keep a chamber pot under the bed. There's a great deal to be said for indoor plumbing.

We have schools that keep costing more and more, true. But for the investment, kids keep coming home smarter and smarter, younger and younger. By the time my youngsters get to junior high school, they know more than I do, and I feel like the fuse that fizzled in the knowledge explosion.

If food prices keep soaring until they're almost out of sight, I try to keep in mind that steak at $1.59 per pound is lots tastier than an empty bowl when the rice is all gone.

Go ahead. Call me corny, but I still get goose-pimples when Old Glory goes by in march time.

And when evening comes, where else in the world can a young feller cuddling with a gal point out into the wild blue yonder and say: "See that moon up there? That's *my* country's flag they planted up there."

By jingy, you can't say that sort of thing anywhere but in America. And if the Boy Scouts can help us to instill an appreciation for this sort of thing in our boys, I say pay the fee, buy the uniform (which will be outgrown before he reaches First Class) and heave to.

Alan plowed right into the middle of it all. Before we had the ink dry on his registration, he had volunteered to carry the flag for a flag-raising ceremony at the crack of dawn one day.

There's this about dawn—it always cracks too early in the springtime.

When the alarm went off at 5:30 A.M., I had just gotten to sleep, having bounced in and out of bed all night once more while Valerie went about her business of cutting teeth.

As soon as the alarm went off, I sprang into action, whipping on my clothes and rushing upstairs to get Alan under way. At least I was under the impression that that was what I was doing, up until the phone rang and I realized that I was still in bed, dreaming that I was springing into action, whipping on my clothes and rushing upstairs to get Alan under way.

The telephone caller was the scoutmaster, wondering where was one flag-bearer, Alan Van Leer by name.

I sprang into action in earnest, and by eliminating everything that wasn't necessary (stockings, lipstick, combing and safety pins to close the gap where a button flew off in the melee) we were out of the house and en route in ten minutes, with myself holding the spot where the safety pin might have been.

When we arrived at the church, the sun was just vaulting up over the horizon. Everything was in readiness. We noted the chairs set in neat semi-circles facing the flagpole. But nobody was sitting in them.

It seems that while the audience sat waiting, sleepy-eyed and foggy, for the flag-bearer to arrive, the automatic watering timer for the church lawn watering system did its duty.

I don't even know if someone said, "Let us spray" first.

That was probably the dampest bunch of patriotic people ever assembled. I was inclined to laugh, but restrained myself, remembering that a Boy Scout's mother is loyal, trustworthy, kind and courteous.

Besides, I realized that many of these, my dear friends, were cleaner and braver than I, having had their morning shower in the brisk breezes by the dawn's early light.

As I told Alan later, it was probably the only thing I'd done wrong right in a long time.

Suppose I'd had him there on time (perish the thought), and he'd been in the process of raising the flag when the sprinklers went into action.

I understand that once the ceremony is begun, one must stick with it until the flag is flying.

On this particular morning, that took a while. Alan put the flag on upside down the first whack.

Only my having slept in kept him from doing his duty standing atop an activated sprinkler. He didn't express any overwhelming gratitude, however.

Later that day, I told the other children how impressive it was, leaving out the part about the audience looking like a gathering of drowned rats.

"I thought it was just lovely," I reported, "with the sun just coming up and the flag flying against the crimson and gold of the sunrise. We ought to be really proud to be Americans."

"Hey, Mom, I know the pledge of allegiance," Russell volunteered. "I learned it on 'Romper Room.' "

"That's wonderful, son. Why don't you say it for us?"

So he did.

"I am allergic to the flag and the United States and America, and to the Republic for which it understands, one nation, under God, invisible, with libraries and juices for all."

I'd say this country is facing some *really* perilous times.

April Showers Make Me
Loony as a June Bug

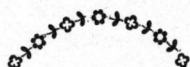

The monsoon season was upon us. Rain fell like sugar crystals into the children's cereal bowls (in a steady stream).

I sat by the window watching the downpour pour down my driveway and into the back yard, where it stopped only long enough to snatch up my newly planted strawberry plants and then go frisking off with them to the neighbors down the block.

"I'll bet those people are probably allergic to strawberries at that." I sighed as they went swishing past.

Nobody, nobody in the whole written history of the world has ever been more poorly done by than I, I noted. Only maybe, possibly, Mrs. Noah. I had great sympathy for her problems:

Noah   (stretching and wringing the water out of his nightcap): Well, good morning, dear. How did you sleep?

Mrs. Noah   Damply. You'll probably go down in biblical history as the first pitch-er who got rained out. Was that really the best quality pitch you could get? The north forty cubits have sprung a leak and all my best linens are getting mildewy.

Noah   Now, Mama.

Mrs. Noah   Don't you "Now, Mama" me. If I'd known it was going to be like this . . . All my life it's been nothing but patter, patter, patter. First all those little feet and now thirty-eight days and thirty-eight nights of this. I can't stand it.

Noah   It can't last much longer, Mama. Be patient.

Mrs. Noah   Be patient! Be patient, he says. How can I be patient when I've got all this livestock tramping through my kitchen all the time? Noah, are you absolutely *positive* that the Lord said to save the boa constrictors and cobras?

Noah   Yes, Mama. Everything. I got two of everything, even the unicorns.

Mrs. Noah   Oh, yes, dear. I've been meaning to bring that up. About those unicorns . . .

Noah   There's nothing wrong with those unicorns, Mama. I've never seen finer specimens. Two handsome, one-horned, great-looking male . . . Oh, oh. Well, I guess that they ain't never gonna see no unicorn.

Mrs. Noah   So don't worry. Anyone could make a little mistake like that. The world will just have to do without unicorns. What I'm worried about, Papa, is how I can keep up the housekeeping with all those crazy animals flitting around. I went over this ark cubit by cubit yesterday, and today you'd never know I lifted a finger. I'll go mad, I tell you.

Noah   Now, Mother. You just calm yourself. This

	rain can't last much longer. Get the daughters-in-law to help with the cleaning.
Mrs. Noah	Ha! Those no-goods. Listen, when we get off this blinkin' ark, those are going to be the three prettiest women in the whole world, at least for a while. Work, yet! They spend more time primping and preening than the blithering peacocks. And those time-frittering, lazy sons of yours. Always clowning around down by the ape cages until I can't tell them from the inmates. It's enough to drive a mother to drink, if you'll pardon the expression.
Noah	All right, all right, dear. I'll put in a little word with the Powers That Be to see if They couldn't turn it off now. In the meantime, why don't you open the window a teensy and shoot one of the doves out to see if he can't find an olive branch or something.
Mrs. Noah	(sighing): Sometimes I wish I'd missed the boat. And believe me, if we overshoot Ararat and come down somewhere in the equatorial rain forest or something, someone's going to hear from me, you can bet!

By golly, I felt better already. I waved a fare-thee-well to the strawberry plants and got into gear to take Valerie and Russell to the doctor for immunizations. Val was in line for another DPT and Russ was in the middle of a polio series.

I left Steven making a cake for dinner and dashed into the downpour with the two little ones, hoping that we wouldn't have too long to wait in Doctor Bob's office.

We were in luck. The office was only lightly packed. Possibly, in view of the drippy weather, some of the patients had decided to take a chance on dying of whatever ailed them rather than taking a chance on getting caught in a flash flood on the way to the doctor's office.

Within a short time, Russ had been dosed and I sent him back to the waiting room while Val had her turn. Then I chatted for a few minutes with Doctor Bob. As it turned out, that was just a few minutes too long.

Having been to the doctor's office before, Russ had come prepared with a bit of something to keep him entertained. He'd had the good sense to keep it pocketed, however, until Mama was safely out of sight in the inner sanctum.

What he'd brought to fend off tedium was a metal tape measure and a small screwdriver.

Naturally enough, he noted right away that a small screw was all that held the tape measure together, all neatly coiled inside the casing.

Since he just happened to have the screwdriver handy anyhow, it was simply a matter of time until he decided to remove the screw and see what would happen.

What happened was that, with a fine metallic *sproinggg,* the tape measure uncoiled all over the doctor's waiting room—about twenty feet of it.

When I hove back onto the scene, there was just a tangled mess of metal tape all over everywhere and a little fellow trying heroically to cram it back into the three-inch casing.

Praise be for diaper bags. I looped the mess up as small as possible and stuffed it in with a warm bottle and three diapers while my fellow patients in the room looked on with unveiled disapproval. I could tell what they were thinking:

"Some people ought to teach their children better."

Oh well. I mustered my dignity and my children and fled willingly into the storm.

When we got home, the older children were having a jolly good time bouncing Steven's cake around the kitchen.

"I don't know what I did wrong, Mom," he said, "but this stuff is just like sponge."

"Not to worry, son," I reassured him. "If the country ever gets cut off from its rubber supply, you'll be a national hero."

"Hey! Maybe I could do it again," he said, reaching for another cake mix.

"Never mind! Never mind!" I halted him in mid-reach. "Let's wait and see if there is ever a real need for it. If there is, I'll be the first to let the government know that you can make rubber from cake mix."

"Just think," he exulted. "We could drive on cake, sleep on cake, wear swimming caps made of cake."

"Marvy," I replied.

"Hey, Mom," Alan cried up from the basement, where he was bouncing cake off the dart board, "Dad called a couple of times. He wants you to call."

I dialed the hospital while shrugging out of my bedewed coat.

"Hi," I said, when I recognized the voice of the lord and master on the other end. "You want me to call?"

"Yep. Listen, are you sure we want to go ahead with this baby business?"

Zounds! He'd changed his mind. After all this time! I prepared to do battle.

"I thought it was all settled. That girl down in California and everything . . ."

"Well, I thought you might change your mind if you knew that they have a five-week-old baby girl at the reservation hospital that we can have."

"You're kidding!"

"Nope. I'm serious."

"You're serious?"

"Serious. They called me this morning. The baby was brought into the hospital last night. Only one thing . . . she was abandoned and they think she was left for about three days. She's suffering from malnutrition and dehydration. We might be taking a chance."

"We were taking a chance on every one of our own. Besides, did anyone ever worry about what kind of chance the child is taking if we adopt it?" I had fallen in love with a baby I hadn't ever seen.

"Don't get defensive, dear. I just think we should think it over a little."

"I just did. I think we ought to take her."

"I thought you would. I told them we'd be after her."

I floated out of the kitchen and into the hallway to hang up my coat.

The rain was still beating on the roof. New baby, new baby, new baby, it said.

Tempus Fugits Like the Dickens

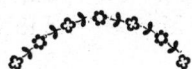

I had hopes that we might get our new baby immediately, but after some more checking, Dirk learned that the hospital wanted to keep the little one for a few days.

She had apparently been left for several days in an old revamped boxcar that the mother was using for a home. They wanted to be sure she was all right before they parted with her.

So I curbed my impatience and prepared to wait a few days longer. After all, I reminded myself every few minutes, if we'd waited for the other baby, it would have been a couple of months longer. It helped, but not much.

In the meantime, I noted again the phenomenon that has occurred to me each time we've looked forward to a new baby, that being that the children who are already with us take on a new perspective.

All of a sudden it seemed the older ones had taken a giant step closer to maturity.

I first became aware of it, I suppose, when I went to put on my girdle and found that the garters had been pre-empted by Laurel, who was using them on the little thingamy she used to keep her long socks up.

Besides that, she was in training these days. A little friend from up the street had given her a "training bra," and she had been wearing it for some time with no noticeable results.

I didn't bother to add to her discouragement by mentioning that I myself had looked like a bed slat until I was almost fourteen.

"You've got years and years yet. Don't be so in a hurry," I told her.

"I'm not. Not really," she assured me in one breath, and in the next asked, "Couldn't you buy me one of those padded slips? They come in sizes seven to fourteen."

"Sorry, sister. If you want to be the Raquel Welch of the fourth grade, you'll have to come by it naturally, even if you're in training for three years."

She sighed and went on about her business, and I noticed a short time later that the training bra had suddenly become the top piece of a two-piece swimming suit for her doll.

Melinda strained at the bit, too, having always resented the fact that her older sister was older than she.

We relented to her strivings toward grown-upness to the extent of letting her go with an older cousin to a church dance while we were visiting. She was to go as a spectator more than as a participant. At least that was the intention.

When she came home a few hours later floating several feet off the floor, we could hardly wait to hear about it.

"I danced every dance," she rejoiced.

"You're kidding!" we exclaimed.

"Nope. I danced every dance," she insisted.

"How come?" we asked.

"Some rich guy was there and he gave the boys a dime for each time they danced with a girl." She sighed.

Of course, we needn't have worried anyhow, Dirk reminded me, that our little preteen was being whirled too soon into the social swing or thrust too early into the arms of the boys.

"The way they dance today, she probably didn't get within a yard of any boy there," he said. "I think the rich guy got rooked."

Even our darling Valerie seemed more grown up. We were convinced that she was the most exceptional child ever born and didn't hesitate to tell everyone so.

I may have mentioned it to Kerma when she strolled over for a visit one morning.

"I read in the newspaper today about a woman in India who has carried her baby for twenty-two months, and not only that, but the baby *talks,*" Kerma noted. "In utero, she does. Not even born yet."

Egad, was this woman casting aspersions on my own superior child?

"Valerie talks too," I replied immediately.

"Oh, sure," Kerma sneered.

"Okay, we'll show you. But let me change her first," I said. "Hand me a diaper out of the diaper bag over there, will you, Kerma?"

She unzipped the diaper bag and twenty feet of metal measuring tape exploded in her face. I had forgotten about that.

"You'd do anything to get me to go home now, wouldn't you?" Kerma accused, untangling herself. "Nothing doing. I'm staying here to hear that baby talk." She tossed me the diaper.

"Sorry about that," I mumbled. "Russell's fault, you know." I busied myself with the diaper change and got my child genius ready for her recital, which I concluded she could recite as I fed her some fruit.

"Well, Tooty," I said, "these are perilous times we live in. Have you come to any conclusions as to your political leanings? I mean, how do you feel about the war, for instance? Are you a hawk or a dove?"

"Coo," she replied.

"See?" I told Kerma.

"Oh, brother. Lct's hear more."

"All right. Now, Valerie, how about pollution? That's a big issue today. What do you have to say about that?"

"Kiki," she responded, knocking the spoon out of my hand and adding to the pollution problems in my kitchen.

"I agree. But would you care to elucidate a bit? If you had to describe the situation in our urban areas, for instance, in one word, could you do it?"

"Gaga," she frowned, choking on her mangled plums.

"Absolutely right, dear," I said, looking up to see how Kerma was taking all this. She was looking out the window. Oh well. I could always talk with Valerie.

"Pollution makes you sick, all right. And here it is another election year. The politicians are already gearing up and it will be mudslinging and name calling for the rest of the year. Have you made up your mind at this stage who you'd like to see in the White House?"

"Mmmmmm."

"Not committing yourself, huh?" I asked. "I'm having trouble myself making up my mind. But there must be someone who'd be better than anyone else. Someone who could straighten out all the messes we seem to be involved in, someone outstanding enough, full of integrity, devoted to duty . . ."

"Dada."

"Yes, of course, sweetheart. But you must realize that your father has other obligations. I'll mention it to him, though. Say, you know, if Daddy can't see his way clear, possibly I could swing it. Hmmm. Wonder how I'd be as the first lady President."

"Bah."

I handed her to Kerma. How can you converse with a kid like that?

Besides, I had a new crisis to deal with.

Russell had concluded that he was now grown up enough to seek his own fortune. He wandered into the kitchen with a paper bag dripping socks and undershirts and announced that he was running away.

I thought it over carefully for two or three seconds and said, "Why not?"

He headed out. In about five minutes he was back.

"Be sure to call me when I'm supposed to go back to Doctor Bob for my other polio stuff," he reminded me.

"Fine, son. Where can I get in touch with you?"

"Oh, probly up at Darin's." (Darin lives three houses away.)

"So long." I cheered him on his way. "Oh, by the way," I added, "this is super dingy [the latest expression going the rounds], because I guess I can have your fudge." I was just mixing up a batch to satisfy the after-school-snack appetites.

"Well, probly maybe I'd better wait until this evening."

By this time he had taken things in and out of his bag so many times that he had to get a new sack in order to be ready to head out right after the fudge. That kept him occupied for the rest of the afternoon, right on through the fudge and on into dinnertime.

It had taken him so long to run away that by now the whole family and most of the neighbor children were involved, telling him where to go and how to get there and how not to miss out on anything special at home while he was doing it.

While he tried to decide on the best course of action, meanwhile rearranging his "going away" bag several hundred times, night fell and he wandered off to bed, vowing to make it first thing in the morning.

I hope so, I thought. I was running out of paper bags.

In the Not-So-Good
Old Summertime

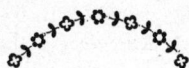

A horrible thing happened a couple of days before B-Day (Baby Day). School let out for the summer.

I must have been expecting it. I know that it happens every summer, but in all the excitement, it had crept up on me unawares. I wasn't psychologically prepared for the summertime routine. I found myself wondering what it was that I had thought was so terrible about wintertime.

If I recalled rightly, it was awfully cold and there were kids underfoot all the time.

But at least I knew where they were at mealtimes. With the advent of summer, there still were kids underfoot all the time—wall-to-wall squirmy flesh of kinfolk and friends from sunrise to sunset—right up until I opened my mouth to say, "Lunch is ready."

Then, somehow, they had disappeared into thin air, and while the sandwiches dried up and the orange juice settled, I wandered through the stilly noon, crying for my lost sheep.

When I finally gave up and went back home, they were sitting at the table devouring the goodies and wondering where I'd been.

The swimming pool around the corner opened, and within a half hour I didn't have a bath towel left. You might say I'd been left high and dry, but somehow that doesn't cover the situation.

When I took my bath, I had two alternatives—jump up and down flapping my arms and gyrating wildly until I created enough wind to dry myself, or else open the window and let the prevailing Montana breeze plaster me securely against the opposite wall for three seconds, in which time I would be not only dry, but blistered and peeling from wind burn.

I'm exaggerating, you know. Actually, at the end of the first day we had several towels—none of which I had ever seen before in my life. I had forgotten, since the last summer, about swimming towels.

I wish someone could explain to me the process by which a child leaves the house toting a perfectly lovely, fluffy new towel with purple flowers on it (I was forced to stock up after the previous swimming season) and returns with a frayed-out, limp, tattletale gray affair that was obviously some other mother's last resort.

What bothered me most was that somewhere in this favored land, there was some happy mother who was whistling after bath and drying herself with my perfectly lovely, fluffy new towel with purple flowers on it.

There was just one solution, and at the end of the first day I advocated it, along with a number of other Rules for Summertime. . . . Let the *kids* gyrate wildly after their swim, or stand out in the breeze to dry. They're younger and can probably gyrate lots better than we more mature folk, I pointed out.

Wandering bath towels, I soon found, were the least of my troubles. As the back yard filled up with youngsters, the decibel count rose alarmingly as they let off all that whoopee-school-is-out steam.

But even with all those decibels running rampant, I recognized a sincere scream of agony when it rent the air.

I tore out of the house and through the garage, noticing

just in the nick of too late that the kids had relocated their little plastic swimming pool to a spot just in front of the garage door.

Dripping from the shirt and slacks and sloshing from the shoes, I continued on my errand of mercy. And it took just a moment to locate the problem.

Russell was screaming at the top of his lungs and holding his right arm, which had a joint in a spot where there had never been one before.

I alerted the hospital emergency room that we were on our way, and within minutes we were hospital-bound, with Alan holding Russell's arm steady on a small pillow to cushion the shocks and bumps.

When we arrived, one of the nurses mistook me for the patient, dripping as I was in a little puddle on the floor. We got that misunderstanding straightened out and they made Russ as comfortable as possible on a bed while we waited for Doctor Bob to arrive.

I must say that after the initial outburst, my little fellow behaved admirably. When Doctor Bob examined the crooked little appendage and suggested X rays, Russell was enthralled.

"My dad owns the X-ray department," he informed one and all.

"You bet he does," the doctor agreed, and we wheeled him down the hall in a wheelchair. He nodded and bowed to everyone we passed, remembering, of course, to make it a bit soulful so that each would be aware that he was there for a purpose and was most likely the most seriously wounded little boy in the annals of Columbus Hospital history.

Dirk was just coming out of the door of his department when we came wheeling up. He didn't say a word, just ushered us through the door and turned himself around to take care of the radiologic honors for his son personally.

It was a nice clean break just above the wrist, and within a short time we were home again, Russell sporting a lovely white cast.

He became an instantaneous sensation in the neighborhood, and before I had my still-dampish clothes changed, the cast had been admired, signatured and generally dirtied up.

Its wearer was in a state of raptured bliss.

"Mom," he said, leaving his fans outside waiting while he got a drink of water, "I think maybe if my arm heals, I'll break the other one, too, this summer."

"Please do that," I replied, wiping my fevered brow. (I realize that I didn't have a fevered brow when this chapter began, but in one day of summer a lot can happen.)

As I mentioned to Dirk that evening when the children were all in bed and the quiet lay around thick as cobwebs: "Isn't it amazing how time flies? Just think, only eighty-nine more days and they'll be back in school."

In Which I Meet Calamity
Head on and Get a Headache

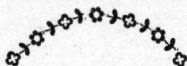

There appeared to have been a leak in our security. Someone had blabbed. News of our impending adoption was
out.

Actually, what happened was that Mom happened to call
on the same day that we had been informed that we could
bring Darlene Marie (the name chosen in agonizing hours
of discussion in which we did a lot of name dropping)
home the next day.

It was too much to ask that I not say anything to my
oldest and dearest friend.

"Mom," I said, "remember all those clues I sent you
about something exciting we were going to do?"

"Don't tell me. You've signed a contract for the Tarzan
bit."

"No, no, no. Not that. We're going to adopt an Indian
baby."

"I thought you would have been great as the background
noises for Tarzan movies."

"It's a little girl, Mom, and we get to pick her up
tomorrow."

There was a short silence. "You really are? Seriously, huh?"

"We've already got her named. She's Darlene Marie."

"Well, that's wonderful. You know that whatever you want is what we want. When will we get to see her?"

Now you know why she's my nominee for Mother of the Year any year.

I had hardly hung up the telephone when it rang again.

What a marvelous instrument, the telephone. One long-distance call and people across half the state knew we were adopting a baby. What I had failed to reckon on were all the little ears sitting around the kitchen listening when Mother called.

As soon as the little ears had picked up the choice tidbit, they had run up and down the neighborhood, dispensing the news to friends near and far. The phone calls poured in as the friends checked on the information and added to the details.

By the time the morning was half over, I had a blister on my ear and a kink in my intentions. I had suddenly remembered that the flannel I bought to make a coming-home outfit for the new member of the family was still upstairs in my sewing box, untouched by human hands since the day it was purchased.

I fled to the sewing machine and set to work, stopping only to answer the phone.

I had almost determined to let the fool thing ring and ignore it while I stuck with the business at hand, when I finally got a call that wasn't someone inquiring were we *really* going to adopt a baby and how come.

The caller on this occasion was an acquaintance from out of town. Her husband was attending a convention and she would just love to visit for a while.

"Marvelous!" I assured her, frantically clutching at every bit of clutter within phone's reach in order not to lose a moment.

"I'll be there in a half hour," she said, and I hung up,

gathered up the kids, shook them out of their summertime lethargy and got them into gear for some quickie house-cleaning without ever losing a stride in my own clutter-gathering campaign.

What with the telephone and the sewing machine going full tilt, the vacuum cleaner and the dishwasher had been totally ignored, but with all of us working, we tore through the house like a whirlwind.

When we got done, it looked as if a whirlwind had passed through.

When I heard the doorbell ring, I grabbed the ironing basket, which was full to overflowing, and threw it in the oven. Then I took two deep breaths and went to the door calm and serene as a summer's day—if a summer day ever got caught carrying a pair of dirty socks.

We had a wonderful visit, regardless, while the friend filled me in on all the news about mutual acquaintances in the town where she lived, which we had vacated about five years earlier for our present location.

While we talked, the children drifted in and out going about their usual business and answering the telephone, which had never ceased ringing. I had them add each new caller to a list of those whom I was to call and explain why in the ever-loving blue-eyed world were we adopting a baby girl.

On one of her passes through the living room, Melinda stopped to pay her respects to the caller.

"Boy, you should have seen us tear through this house cleaning up when we heard you were coming," she said. "Mom threw Dad's underwear in the closet, and the ironing basket is in the oven."

It is to weep.

When Brian shuffled over to get his licks in, I held my breath.

However, the caller forestalled any fiasco on his part by pouring on the flattery.

"You've really grown into a handsome young man, Brian," she said. "You know, you were just a little fellow when you moved. I'll bet you're really a good boy and do everything your mother asks you to do."

Poor Brian. Caught between his natural inclination to accept all this praise and our constant admonition to always tell the truth.

"Well," he hedged, "sometimes my mother calls me an ass and a wretched child."

Our visit didn't last much longer, fortunately or otherwise. Much as I'd like to have heard more about the old home town, I still had a receiving blanket and nightie in the about-half-done stages and dinner upcoming.

I flipped on the oven to preheat for baked potatoes, and went back to the sewing machine upstairs.

Somehow I kept on going one seam longer, and when my project got so far along it would take just a few more minutes, I spent another half hour and finished. I had just little touches of lace to add when Steve burst upstairs.

"Hey, Mom!" he screeched. "Something terrible is burning in the oven. It smells awful."

I whipped down the stairs three at a time and flung open the oven door. Too late, too late. My nice sturdy ironing basket was disintegrating before my very eyes and some of the clothes were beginning to toast. The odor was odiferous.

I grabbed a newspaper and threw the whole mess out of the oven onto the paper, then snatched the clothes out and threw them ·into a heap on the kitchen floor. Only a few items were melted to the plastic beyond saving.

When Dirk got home, I was scraping plastic off my oven rack. The oven had cooled but I hadn't.

"Hi. What's for dinner?" he asked, apparently unable to notice that only my tail feathers were visible, the rest of me being entombed in the oven.

"Nothing," I said.

"What?" he asked.

I pulled my head out of the oven long enough to say, "Nothing," again, and went back to work.

"You mean nothing at all?" he asked.

"Nothing whatsoever," I assured him. "However, don't get too upset, because with any luck at all, we may have breakfast tomorrow morning."

"That kind of a day?" he observed.

"Worse."

"Hmmm. Well, what say that we celebrate the Day Before Adoption and take the kids out for hamburgers."

"Whoopee!" I yelled, becoming one of an octet.

I had forgotten the last time we went out to eat, which is just as well.

The man who advocated togetherness for families has never been together with my family at a restaurant. (It had to be a man. No woman in her right mind would suggest togetherness for any social occasion, barring a Swedish bath.)

Be that as it may, we went, choosing a nice family-type restaurant where we were seated around the corner and toward the back, either by chance or on purpose.

We didn't have a bit of trouble until we sat down. Then Russell knocked over his ice water, which ran off the table into Laurie's lap. I grabbed some napkins and leaned across the table to salvage the situation the best I could, and didn't realize until I felt something cool and moist running down my leg that I was lying atop my own glass of ice water.

There didn't seem to be much point in fighting it, so I just lay there and let the water soak into the front of my dress.

While I soaked up water, Dirk gave the waitress our order, and in due time we settled down to the serious business of reducing things to crumbs.

Since I happened to have been delegated to hold Valerie (for a change), everyone was finished when I hadn't yet touched fork to pie. So Laurel, bless her, volunteered to juggle little sister while I finished.

It was at this juncture that we learned that around the corner and toward the back was not necessarily the best place for our family to be. For it was here that the fire exit was located.

We became terribly aware of it when buzzers buzzed and bells clanged right after Laurel leaned against the bar across the door to prop herself up a little, triggering the fire alarm.

Once the other diners realized that the only fires around were those burning in Dirk's cheeks and mine, they settled back for a good chuckle while they tried to figure out if we had been attempting to skip out the fire exit without paying for the goodies or simply had an accident. I imagine the vote was about equally divided.

While they chuckled and laid their bets, the alarm went on alarming. The waitress tried to turn it off and couldn't. So she called the cook, who tried to turn it off and couldn't, so he called in the manager, who finally mustered some blessed quiet.

"Oh, well," I told Dirk. "We don't ever have to go back there. There are plenty of other restaurants around and we can try another one sometime."

"Sure. I think 1983 will be about soon enough."

That night in bed, I thought it over.

"You know, there's something to be learned from all this," I said to Dirk.

"Of course there is. We won't do it again."

"No, I don't mean that. I mean that an experience like this should be shared with others who could benefit from it."

"Like who could that possibly be?"

"You take all the high school seniors who were gradu-ated this past week. There they are, turned out to face the world totally unprepared. Now, if we could have them take turns taking our children out to dinner just once each, what an education that would be. They'd be ready for anything, including an invasion of crocodiles."

"Sometimes I get the idea that you don't really like children," he accused.

"Sometimes I don't."

"I'm going to tell the judge that when we see him tomorrow."

"You do and I'll hide your can of fishing worms."

"Peace, sister."

"Peace to you, too. And good night."

THE Day—B-Day

My eyes popped open and I looked at the clock. I could have sworn it said four o'clock. Then I focused a little better and I really could have sworn, because the clock *did* say four o'clock and I was wide awake.

I closed my eyes again and willed myself to sleep. After an hour or so I opened them and looked at the clock. It said four-fifteen. What a day to have the clock go whacky! I threw back the covers and headed for the kitchen to check with the clock in there. It said four-fifteen too. Imagine! A veritable rash of clock troubles.

I stood there on one bare foot and thought it over. I was up, wasn't I? No doubt about it—there was sugar on my bare foot, and that rarely happens in bed, but it happens regularly in our kitchen. I was up.

And the ironing I had been going to get to yesterday was right there staring me in my blinky eyes, wasn't it? I plugged in the iron. It was obvious that my sleeping was done for the night and I might just as well be doing something worth while.

I had ironed for about a half hour before the first child drifted into the kitchen.

"Have you got the new baby yet?" Brian asked, blinking in the glare of the kitchen light.

"Not yet, son. It isn't even daylight. Hike on back to bed."

"Okay, but I think I'll have a bowl of cereal first."

I suppose it was the sound of cereal soaking up milk that brought Russell trudging into the kitchen. He sat down at the table without a word and spent a pleasant interlude looking at his cast.

A grumpy "What's going on here?" heralded the arrival of Laurel and Melinda.

"When are you going after Darlene Marie?" Melinda asked, pouring cereal into a bowl.

"We aren't leaving until seven," I said. "Why don't you all get back into bed?" It was four forty-five.

Alan and Steve didn't make it for another ten minutes. They joined the groggy throng at the table, and the cereal and milk changed hands again. I ironed and they ate, and then I ironed while they lounged around the table just mostly looking at one another. Russ fell asleep again, his head cradled on his cast. Brian stretched out on two chairs and hummed.

By six-thirty, when Dirk staggered into the kitchen yawning and scratching his head, the girls were asleep on the living-room floor, Brian was still on two chairs, Russ still pillowed on his cast at the table, the ironing basket was half empty and Alan and Steve were getting Valerie ready for another day.

"Where you been all day?" I asked.

Poor friend hubby simply gave it all another glance and then disappeared into the bathroom. I put the iron and ironing board away and went to get dressed.

B-Day had dawned . . . a dripping, drizzling day, to be sure . . . but it had dawned.

A half hour later, we left amid echoing cries of "Don't be gone long," and "Hurry up with that baby." The baby sitter waved us off as we rounded the corner to the tune of the sweeping windshield wipers.

The schedule called for us to stop first in the county seat of the county from which we were getting our baby girl. We had to see the judge there before going on some thirty miles to the town where the little one was hospitalized.

As the miles slished past, silence hung comfortably in the air. Both Dirk and I were wrapped in our own thoughts about this new adventure.

Getting a baby of your own is one thing. This was a whole new kettle of cod. All the weeks and months that we had waited I think I hadn't quite believed that it would ever come to pass, and my mind was full to overflowing with all the questions, thoughts and emotions I'd been building up.

What would she be like? Suppose we didn't love her as much as we did the other children? What sort of problems were we letting ourselves in for? How come we didn't turn around and go back home?

We didn't, though. Mile passed mile in orderly succession, and in due time we were parked at the courthouse.

The lawyer we had hired long-distance at the recommendation of a friend met us inside. Any minute now we'd be the parents, legally, of that little person who had existed in our hearts and minds for the past week.

Our hopes died a-borning, as it were.

"We've got a little problem," the lawyer informed us. "The natural mother skipped out without signing a release. I'm sure we can find her, but it might be a little while. Why don't you look around town while I go looking. And don't worry, this is a small town. She can't be far."

I was crestfallen. All of this business was supposed to have been completed. (And would have been, I knew, except for the fact that motherhood doesn't step aside easily. The mother had gone to the hospital willing to sign a release so that her child could be put into another home, but apparently had not been able to find the courage to put her signature to paper when the time came. She left the hospital and now had obviously gone into hiding.)

My heart went out to her again just as it had many, many times in the past few months, even though I could have no idea who "she" might be. Surely no woman could part with her child without regrets, even when she realized that she couldn't care for it properly.

The lawyer was right. It was a small town. We went to the local hotel and had an early lunch, since neither of us had taken time for breakfast.

We strolled up and down the business section, stopped in a dime store and bought a little toy for each of the youngsters at home. We sat in the car in front of the courthouse and watched the traffic pass.

The lawyer, a most kind and considerate man, returned to report no progress, but he invited us to pass some time at his home, which we did, visiting with his wife and four youngsters. With each minute that passed, my heart sank further, and as the hours piled on top of each other, I knew that we were going to go home empty-handed.

Which all goes to prove that I don't know much. Just when I had reached the depths of despair, the lawyer returned with the signed papers. Oh, me of little faith!

The formalities at the courthouse were over quickly. Normally there is a six-month waiting period in Montana before an adoption is final. The judge waived the waiting period for us with the comment that, "Anyone with eight children who comes looking for another one doesn't have to wait."

If and when we finally got that baby, she would be ours completely. We showered the judge with thanks, the lawyer with thanks, blew kisses at the courthouse and headed the car toward the reservation hospital where Darlene Marie slept, no doubt, all unaware that she was "family" now.

In every mother's memory there is a special niche for the

moment that marks the birth of each new child, never to be forgotten. With Darlene, that special moment was when the nurses took us to the room where she was sleeping and let us go in alone to dress her and get her ready to go home.

She was so teeny, weeny tiny, she was almost lost in the middle of the large crib, and she was wrapped in a gray blanket which I thought sickly was dirty, but Dirk assured me it was just gray—government issue, like all the blankets here.

I could hardly wait to get her into the yellow nightie and her own special blanket. And what a fortunate choice it turned out to be. The yellow made a perfect backstop for the black hair that covered her tiny head in a thick, long carpet, and for the sweet little face that drew up into a frown as we disturbed her slumbers.

Possibly she wasn't as adorable as we thought she was. But let's be fair. The nurses all raved as we showed her off up and down the corridor. She must have been adorable, or why would they have done that?

For more than two hours, as we retraced our journey, I didn't take my eyes off her, except at intervals to check to be sure that Dirk had *his* eyes on the road. Most often he did, but I caught him several times peeking our way.

How strange, how strange! She had been only a thought, a hope, a vague yearning for all the time we had known about her, and now she was a living, breathing, squirming, wiggly real-for-sure human being.

Our hearts grew two sizes larger, and that was just enough, because she was so very small.

Because we had been delayed so long at the county seat, we knew that the children would be having the itchy fidgets waiting for us to get home.

We were right. When we pulled into the driveway, they literally burst out of the house through both doors and swamped us before we could get out of the car.

The Inquiring, Admiring and Aspiring Society was in

session, and the main business at hand was to inquire how come we were so late, to admire the new little sister and to aspire to be the first to hold her.

We moved the meeting into the house and introduced the baby to each of the children in turn, letting them look, hug, kiss and trundle just as long as the next one in line would allow.

When it came Steve's turn, he buried his nose in her neck and crooned.

"My word!" he exclaimed, emerging with a surprised look on his face. "I don't think this baby is adopted. She smells just as sweet as Valerie."

Darlene Marie was home.

About the Title
(in Case You Were Wondering)

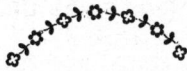

One day, when a friend and I were having a quiet conversation (we weren't at my house) and discussing little bits of this and that, she happened to remark:

"You've brought so much life into the world, you must have some sort of profound philosophy about life."

"Oh," said I without thinking much (as is my wont), "I do, I do. I think life is just a bowl of kumquats."

My friend looked properly puzzled and said, "What do you mean? I don't know what kumquats are."

"I don't either," I replied. "Nor do I know what life is. It's such a terribly individual thing that I believe it's impossible to generalize about it."

"Oh," she commented.

"I mean," I continued, "that to me, the individual human being is the sum and substance of it all, but then, my opinion has never carried a great deal of weight."

"I see," she said.

I am still trying to figure out if she meant "I see that your opinion doesn't carry much weight," or "I see that the individual human being is the sum and substance of it all."